Beginning
MEAN Stack
(MongoDB, Express, Angular, Node.js)

Greg Lim

FIRST EDITION: AUGUST 2021

TECHNICAL EDITOR: DANIEL CORREA

Table of Contents

PREFACE

About this book

In this book, we take you on a fun, hands-on and pragmatic journey to learning MEAN stack development. You'll start building your first MEAN stack app within minutes. Every chapter is written in a bite-sized manner and straight to the point as I don't want to waste your time (and most certainly mine) on the content you don't need. In the end, you will have the skills to create a Movies review app and deploy it to the Internet.

In the course of this book, we will cover:

The goal of this book is to teach you MEAN stack development in a manageable way without overwhelming you. We focus only on the essentials and cover the material in a hands-on practice manner for you to code along.

Working Through This Book

This book is purposely broken down into short chapters where the development process of each chapter will center on different essential topics. The book takes a practical hands on approach to learning through practice. You learn best when you code along with the examples in the book.

Requirements

No previous knowledge on Node.js or Angular development is required, but you should have basic programming knowledge. It will be a helpful advantage if you could read through my Node, Express book and Angular book first which will provide you will better insight and deeper knowledge into the various technologies. But even if you have not done so, you should still be able to follow along.

Getting Book Updates

To receive updated versions of the book, subscribe to our mailing list by sending a mail to support@i-ducate.com. I try to update my books to use the latest version of software, libraries and will update the codes/content in this book. So, do subscribe to my list to receive updated copies!

Code Examples

You can obtain the source code of the completed project at www.greglim.co/p/mean.

CHAPTER 1: INTRODUCTION

Welcome to Beginning MEAN Stack! This book focuses on the key tasks and concepts to get you started to learn and build MEAN stack applications in a faster pace. It is designed for readers who don't need all the details about MEAN at this point in the learning curve but concentrate on what you really need to know.

So what's the MEAN stack? The MEAN stack is a popular stack of technologies for building a modern Single Page Application. MEAN stands for MongoDB, Express, Angular and Node.js:

- Node.js is one of the most popular server-side frameworks that allow us to execute JavaScript code in a web server.
- Express is a web application framework for Node.js which makes application development in Node easier and faster. Node and Express together form the middle-tier web server of the stack.
- MongoDB is a NoSQL database which stores data persistently in the form of collections and documents.
- Angular is a frontend framework to build user interfaces.

Another popular stack variant is the MERN where we use React as the frontend. These frontends make up Single Page Applications (SPAs) which avoid reloading the page entirely and just fetches relevant portions of the page from the server to display new content.

The App We Will Be Building

We will build a Movie reviews app which lets users view and search for movies. They can also log in and post reviews on the movies (fig. 1a, 1b, 1c).

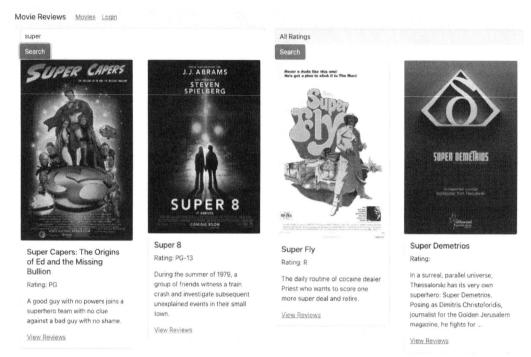

Figure 1a – Home Page with search functionality

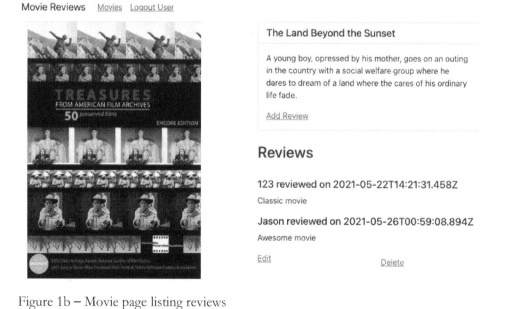

Figure 1b – Movie page listing reviews

Movie Reviews   Movies   Logout User

Create Review

Enjoyed it!

Submit

Figure 1c – Create Review

Users can see the list of reviews in a Movie's page and post/edit/delete their own review if they are logged in. They will not be able edit/delete other's reviews though. Through this app, we will learn a lot of concepts and solidify our Node.js, Express, Angular and MongoDB knowledge.

We will first talk about MongoDB and how to host our database in the cloud using MongoDB Atlas. We will then create the backend of the app using Node.js and Express. Our server will interact with the database using the native MongoDB JavaScript library. After that, we will create the frontend with Angular and connect the frontend to the backend to complete our MEAN stack app. In the last chapter, we will deploy our Node, Express backend on Heroku, and Angular frontend on Netlify, to run both backend and frontend in the cloud.

So, the overall structure of our app will be:
- the 'M' of the stack, MongoDB will be hosted on MongoDB Atlas.
- the 'E' and 'N' , Express and Node runs the backend server (Express being part of Node) and exposes an API. Hosted on Heroku.
- the 'A', Angular frontend calls the API and renders the user interface on the client's browser. Hosted on Netlify.

We will begin by going through the MongoDB database layer in the next chapter.

CHAPTER 2: MONGODB OVERVIEW

As indicated by the 'M' in MEAN, we will use MongoDB as the backend database for our app. MongoDB is a NoSQL database. Before we talk about what is a NoSQL database, let's first talk about relational databases so that we can provide a meaningful contrast. If you have not heard of a relational database before, you can think of relational databases like spreadsheets where data is structured and each entry is generally a row in a table. Relational databases are generally controlled with SQL or Structured Query Language. Examples of popular relational databases are MySQL, SQL Server and PostgreSQL.

NoSQL databases in contrast are often called non-relational databases, where NoSQL means anything that isn't an SQL (see how it infers the popularity of SQL?). It might seem like NoSQL is a protest over SQL but it actually refers to a database not structured like a spreadsheet, i.e. less rigid than SQL databases.

The architecture of MongoDB is a NoSQL database which stores information in the form of *collections* and *documents*. MongoDB stores one or more *collections*. A *collection* represents a single entity in our app, for example in an e-commerce app, we need entities like categories, users, products. Each of these entities will be a single *collection* in our database.

If we were to map similar concepts in relational databases and MongoDB:
- a *table* in a relational database would compare to a *collection* in MongoDB.
- each row in a table (in a relational database) can be thought of as a *document* in a collection (in MongoDB).
- a *join* operation in SQL can be done with *$lookup* in MongoDB.
- instead of foreign keys, we utilize *reference* in MongoDB.

In MongoDB, a *collection* contains *documents*. A *document* is an instance of the entity containing the various relevant field values to represent the *document*. For example, a product *document* will contain title, description and price fields. Each field is a *key-value* pair e.g. `price: 26, title: "Learning Node"`.

Documents look a lot like JSON objects with various properties (though they are technically Binary JSON or BSON). An example of a *collection-document* tree is shown below:

```
Database
   → Products collection
      → Product document
            {
               price: 26,
               title: "Learning Node",
               description: "Top Notch Development book",
               expiry date: 27-3-2020
            }
      → Product document
      ...
   → Users collection
      → User document
            {
               username: "123xyz",
               contact:
                  {
                     phone: "123-456-7890",
                     email: "xyz@example.com"
                  }
            }
      → User document
      ...
```

You can see in the above that we have a variety of relationships. A user has a username and contact. Within contact, you have phone and email. The BSON format provides for a wide variety of support for data types like strings, integers etc.

Let's create our database in the next chapter.

CHAPTER 3: SETTING UP MONGODB ATLAS CLOUD DATABASE

The fastest and easiest way to get started with MongoDB is by using its cloud service MongoDB Atlas to host our database on the cloud. One way of setting up MongoDB is by running MongoDB on a local machine for development and testing. But MongoDB Atlas makes things a lot easier even if we are just doing a local project. Also, our entire backend and frontend will eventually be deployed to the cloud anyway.

First, sign up for a MongoDB Atlas account (https://www.mongodb.com/download-center). Under 'Deploy a free cluster', create a new account and click 'Get started free' (fig. 1).

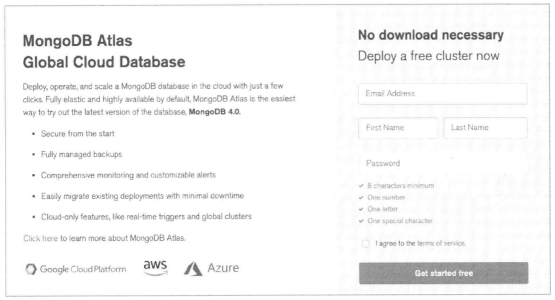

Figure 1

You will be brought to a 'Build a New Cluster' page. Under 'Global Cluster Configuration', choose 'AWS' as cloud provider (because they provide a free account without having to enter credit card details). Under 'North America', select 'North Virginia' where we can get a free tier for our MongoDB (fig. 2).

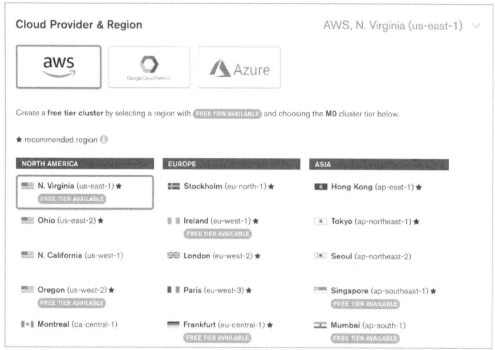

Figure 2

Next under 'Cluster Tier', choose the 'M0' free tier (fig. 3).

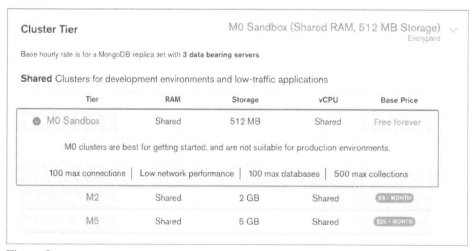

Figure 3

The good thing about Amazon AWS is that we can experiment without having to worry about making unintentional mistakes and getting a huge bill from Amazon. When your website gets more popular with more users, you can then scale up at a later stage. Keep the other default options and select 'Create Cluster.' It will prompt you saying that it takes 7-10 minutes to set up everything on AWS (fig. 4).

Figure 4

Next, in the left panel, under 'Security', click on 'Database Access' where you do not yet have a user. Create a database user by clicking on 'Add New User' (fig. 5) and provide him with 'Read and write to any database privileges'.

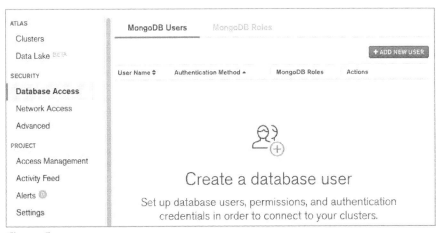

Figure 5

Next, under 'Security', 'Network Access', 'IP Whitelist', select 'Add IP Address' and choose 'allow access from anywhere' (fig. 6). This will allow our app to be accessible from anywhere in the Internet.

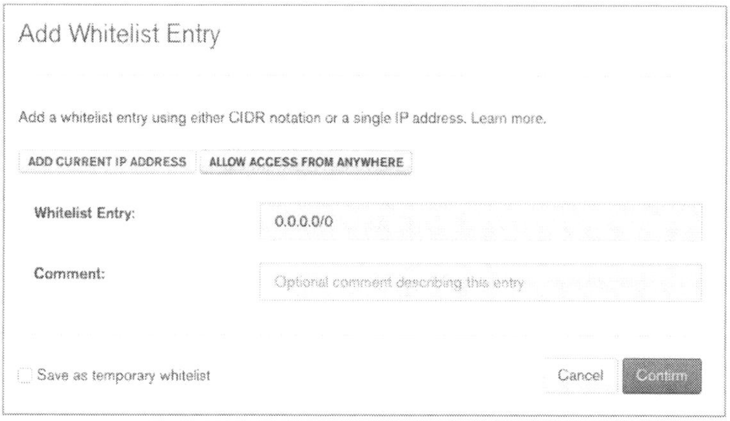

Figure 6

We will later revisit the MongoDB site to retrieve the connection string to connect MongoDB and our Node.js backend. For now, let's add some sample data to our database.

Chapter 4: Adding Sample Data

One thing great about MongoDB is when you want some dummy data to try things out, you don't have to painstakingly generate your own data. MongoDB provides a lot of sample data for us. In the MongoDB Cluster, click on the three dots '...' and select 'Load sample Dataset' (fig. 1). This will load a sample dataset into your cluster.

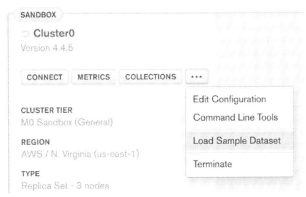

Figure 1

To see the sample data, click on 'Collections', and you see a list of sample databases e.g. 'sample_mflix', 'sample_analytics' (fig. 2).

sample_airbnb

sample_analytics

sample_geospatial

sample_mflix

sample_restaurants

sample_supplies

sample_training

sample_weatherdata

Figure 2

In our app, we will use the 'sample_mflix' data. *sample_mflix* contains movies' data (fig. 3).

Figure 3

For example, in the first listing, we have the 'The Poor Little Rich Girl' movie. We have the movie's runtime, title, plot, year and more. We will use these data in our app.

Having loaded our sample data, let's start creating our backend in the next chapter.

CHAPTER 5: SETTING UP OUR NODE.JS, EXPRESS BACKEND

In this chapter, we begin setting up the backend of our app with Node.js and Express. First, we will install Node.js. Go to *nodejs.org* (fig. 1) and download the appropriate version for your Operating System.

Figure 1

Installation should be straightforward. Once Node.js has been installed, go to your Terminal and run:

```
node -v
```

This shows the version of Node that you installed e.g. *v14.16.0* (at time of this book's writing).

Creating the Backend folder

In Terminal, in a location of your choice, create a folder called 'movie-reviews' e.g.:

```
mkdir movie-reviews
cd movie-reviews
```

In the *movie-reviews* folder, create a folder called 'backend':

```
mkdir backend
cd backend
```

In the *backend* folder, create a *package.json* file in the folder by running:

```
npm init
```

This will prompt a series of questions about our project (e.g. project name, author, version) to create *package.json* for us. You can of course manually create *package.json* on your own. But *npm init* saves us a bit of time when creating *package.json* files. For now, press enter for the first three questions, in the 'entry point' question write *Index.js*, and press enter for the rest of the questions. At the end, *package.json* (with the contents something like the below) will be generated for us.

```
{
  "name": "backend",
  "version": "1.0.0",
  "description": "",
  "main": "Index.js",
  "scripts": {
    "test": "echo \"Error: no test specified\" && exit 1"
  },
  "author": "",
  "license": "ISC"
}
```

package.json contains metadata about our Node project like the name, version and its authors.

Next, install a few dependencies by running:

```
npm install express cors mongodb dotenv
```

As mentioned, *Express* is a framework that acts as a light layer atop the Node.js web server making it easier to develop Node.js web applications. It simplifies the APIs of Node.js, adds helpful features, helps organizes our application's functionality with middleware and routing and many others.

CORS stands for Cross-Origin Resource Sharing. By default, modern browsers don't allow frontend clients to talk to REST APIs. They block requests sent from clients to the server as a security mechanism to make sure that client-side browser JavaScript code can only talk to their own allowed server and not to some other servers which can potentially run malicious code. To circumvent this security mechanism, we can enable CORS checking, a mechanism that uses additional HTTP headers to tell browsers to give a web application running at one origin, access to selected resources from a different origin.
The *cors* package we are installing provides an Express middleware that can enable CORS with different options so we can make the right connections on the network.

The *mongodb* dependency allows us to interact with our MongoDB database.

The *dotenv* dependency loads environmental variables from the *process.env* file instead of setting environment variables on our development machine which simplifies development. We will understand this better when we create the *process.env* file later.

When installation of the above dependencies is finished, you will notice that a new property *dependencies* has been added to *package.json*.

```
{
  "name": "backend",
  "version": "1.0.0",
  "description": "",
  "main": "Index.js",
  "scripts": {
    "test": "echo \"Error: no test specified\" && exit 1"
  },
  "author": "",
  "license": "ISC",
  "dependencies": {
    "cors": "^2.8.5",
    "dotenv": "^10.0.0",
    "express": "^4.17.1",
    "mongodb": "^4.1.0"
  }
}
```

Dependencies contain the dependency packages and their version numbers. For example, we have Express version 4.17.1 (at time of book's writing). Each time we install a package, *npm* saves it here to keep track of the packages used in our app.

npm install installs the specified packages into our app by fetching their latest versions and putting them in a folder called *node_modules*. Open up the *backend* folder in a code editor of your choice. In this book, I will be using Visual Studio Code (https://code.visualstudio.com/).

If you look at your app folder, the *node_modules* folder will have been created for you (fig. 2). This is where custom dependencies are saved for our project.

Figure 2

If you open and explore *node_modules*, you should be able to locate the *installed* packages. The reason why we see many other packages in *node_modules* is because our specified packages depend on these other packages and they were thus also installed. The file *package-lock.json* tracks the versions of all the dependencies of Express.

Automatic Server Restart with nodemon

Next, we will install a package called *nodemon* (https://www.npmjs.com/package/nodemon) that automatically detects code changes and restart the Node server so we don't have to manually stop and restart it whenever we make a code change. Install *nodemon* with the following command:

```
npm install -g nodemon
```

And *nodemon* will be installed globally to our system path.

CHAPTER 6: CREATING OUR BACKEND SERVER

Now, its time to create the backend server! But before we do, because we are using ES6's *import* statement, add into *package.json* the below line:

```
{
  "name": "backend",
  "version": "1.0.0",
  "description": "",
  "main": "Index.js",
  "type": "module",
  "scripts": {
    "test": "echo \"Error: no test specified\" && exit 1"
  },
...
```

That will use the *import* statements from ES6.

Now, in the *backend* folder, create a new file *Index.js* with the following code:

```
import express from 'express';
import cors from 'cors';
import MoviesRoute from './api/MoviesRoute.js';

class Index {
  static app = express();

  static router = express.Router();

  static main() {
    Index.setUpServer();
  }

  static setUpServer() {
    Index.app.use(cors());
    Index.app.use(express.json());
```

```
     Index.app.use('/api/v1/movies',
MoviesRoute.configRoutes(Index.router));
     Index.app.use('*', (req, res) => {
       res.status(404).json({ error: 'not found' });
     });
   }
}


Index.main();
```

Code Explanation

```
import express from 'express';
import cors from 'cors';
import MoviesRoute from './api/MoviesRoute.js';
```

We first import the *express* and *cors* middleware. We also import *MoviesRoute.js* which is a separate file we will create later to store our movies routes. We then create an Index class. This will be our entry point to the application. The Index class contains the next elements:

A static attribute called *app*, which creates the server:

```
static app = express();
```

Another static attribute called *router*, which provides access to express router:

```
static router = express.Router();
```

A static method called *main()* to define the application flow of execution. For now, we only invoke another method called *setUpServer()*:

```
static main() {
  Index.setUpServer();
}
```

setUpServer() configures the server execution. In it, we attach the *cors* and *express.json* middleware that express will use with:
```
Index.app.use(cors());
Index.app.use(express.json());
```

express.json is the JSON parsing middleware to enable the server to read and accept JSON in a request's body.

Note: Middleware are functions that Express executes in the middle after the incoming request and before the output. Middlewares might make changes to the request and response objects. The *use* function registers a middleware with our Express app. With *Index.app.use(express.json())*, the *express.json()* middleware let's us retrieve data from a request via the *body* attribute. We shall see this in code later on. Without this middleware, data retrieval would be much more difficult.

We then specify the initial routes:

```
Index.app.use('/api/v1/movies', MoviesRoute.configRoutes(Index.router));
Index.app.use('*', (req, res) => {
  res.status(404).json({ error: 'not found' });
});
```

The general convention for API urls is to begin it with: */api/<version number>*. And since our API is about movies, the main URL for our app will be i.e. *localhost:5000/api/v1/movies*. The subsequent specific routes are specified in the 2nd argument *MoviesRoute.configRoutes(Index.router)*.

If someone tries to go to a route that doesn't exist, the wild card route *Index.app.use('*')* returns a 404 page with the 'not found' message.

```
Index.main();
```

We then invoke the *Index.main()* static method, to initialize the application execution.

Storing Environment Variables

Before we create the file that connects to the database and starts the server, we will create the *env* file to store our environment variables. Create a new file *.env*. This is where we will set the URI of our database. To get the URI, we have to go back to MongoDB Atlas. Once there, click on *connect* (fig. 1).

Figure 1

Under 'Choose a connection method', choose 'connect your application' and copy the URL (fig. 2).

Figure 2

Go back to the *.env* file and declare a variable MOVIEREVIEWS_DB_URI and assign the copied URL to it as shown in the following code:

```
MOVIEREVIEWS_DB_URI=mongodb+srv://newuser1:pwd123@cluster0.vxjpr.mongodb.net/sample_mflix?retryWrites=true&w=majority
```

Make sure in the connect string that you have filled in your own username (e.g. 'newuser1'), password (e.g. 'pwd123') and database name ('sample_mflix').

We will create another two variables in *.env*:

```
MOVIEREVIEWS_NS=sample_mflix // our database name
PORT=5000 // starting port of server
```

Connecting to Database and Start Server

Modify the *Index.js* file, we will connect to the database and start the server. Fill in *Index.js* with the following in **bold**:

```
import express from 'express';
import cors from 'cors';
import MoviesRoute from './api/MoviesRoute.js';
import dotenv from 'dotenv';
import mongodb from 'mongodb';

class Index {
  ...

  static main() {
    dotenv.config();
    Index.setUpServer();
    Index.setUpDatabase();
  }

  static setUpServer() {
    ...
  }

  static async setUpDatabase() {
    const client = new
mongodb.MongoClient(process.env.MOVIEREVIEWS_DB_URI);
    const port = process.env.PORT || 8000;
    try {
      // Connect to the MongoDB cluster
      await client.connect();
      Index.app.listen(port, () => {
        console.log(`server is running on port:${port}`);
      });
    } catch (e) {
      console.error(e);
      process.exit(1);
    }
  }
}

Index.main();
```

Code Explanation

```
import dotenv from 'dotenv';
import mongodb from 'mongodb';
```

First, we import *mongodb* to access our database and *dotenv* to access our environment variables.

We modify the *main()* static method to call **dotenv.config()** to load in the environment variables. We also invoke the *setUpDatabase()* static method.

```
static async setUpDatabase() {
  ...
}
```

We create an asynchronous static method *setUpDatabase()* to connect to our MongoDB cluster, call functions that access our database, and start the server.

```
const client = new mongodb.MongoClient(process.env.MOVIEREVIEWS_DB_URI);
```

In the above, we create an instance of *MongoClient* and pass in the database URI.

```
const port = process.env.PORT || 8000;
```

We retrieve the port from our environment variable. If we can't access it, we use port 8000.

```
        await client.connect();
```

In the *try* block, we then call *client.connect* to connect to the database. *client.connect()* returns a promise. We use the *await* keyword to indicate that we block further execution until that operation has completed.

After connecting to the database and there are no errors, we then start our web server with:

```
        Index.app.listen(port, () => {
          console.log(`server is running on port:${port}`);
        });
```

Index.app.listen starts the server and listens via the specified port. The callback function provided in the 2nd argument is executed when the server starts listening. In our case, when the server starts, it logs a message 'server is running on port:5000' for example.

We wrap our calls to functions that interact with the database in a *try/catch* statement so that we handle any unexpected errors.

```
Index.main();
```

With the *main()* static method implemented, we then call it to execute the application.

We can then test the backend server. But first, we need to make a route.

Creating our first route

In the *backend* folder, create a new directory called *api*. In it, create a new file *MoviesRoute.js*. We have referenced this in *Index.js*. Fill it in with the following:

```
export default class MoviesRoute {
  static configRoutes(router) {
    router.route('/').get((req, res) => res.send('hello world'));
    return router;
  }
}
```

Code Explanation

MoviesRoute.js will contain routes that different people can go to. For now, we just have one route '/' acting as a demonstration. The *configRoutes(router)* static method uses the express router defined in the *Index.js* file to add routes to the express router. We will add more routes later. So, if you go to *localhost:8000/api/v1/movies*, you should get a response with 'hello world'. This is because in *Index.js*, we imported *MoviesRoute.js* and specified the following path:

```
import MoviesRoute from './api/MoviesRoute.js';

...
Index.app.use('/api/v1/movies', MoviesRoute.configRoutes(Index.router));
...
```

Thus, every route defined in the *MoviesRoute.js* file will start with `/api/v1/movies`.

Running our App

In Terminal, *cd* to the *backend* directory and run *nodemon server* to test run your app and it should print out the message:

```
server is running on port:5000
```

If you didn't get any errors, it means you have successfully connected to the database (a common error is putting in a wrong password in the connection string). We are not accessing anything in the database yet, but we are at least connected to the database.

Note: You may see a deprecation warning something like:

```
"Warning: Current Server Discovery and Monitoring engine is deprecated,
and will be removed in a future version. To use the new Server Discover
and Monitoring engine, pass option { useUnifiedTopology: true } to the
MongoClient constructor."
```

It is fine to leave them there, but you can remove them by passing options to the *MongoClient*. For example, you could instantiate *MongoClient* by adding:

```
new mongodb.MongoClient(
        process.env.MOVIEREVIEWS_DB_URI,
        { useNewUrlParser: true, useUnifiedTopology: true }
);
```

See the Node.js MongoDB Driver API documentation for more information on these options.

Now, go to the browser and type in the URL *localhost:5000/api/v1/movies* and it should print out the following:

hello world

Figure 1

This shows that our route is working. And if you enter any other URL, like http://localhost:5000/123, you will get the error:

```
{"error":"not found"}
```

Which is returned by the wild card route:

```
Index.app.use('*', (req, res) => {
  res.status(404).json({ error: 'not found' });
});
```

CHAPTER 7: CREATING THE MOVIES DATA ACCESS OBJECT

Next, we will implement the movies data access object to allow our code to access movie(s) in our database. So in *backend* directory, create a directory called *dao* (data access object).

In *dao*, create the file *MoviesDAO.js* with the following code:

```
export default class MoviesDAO {
  static movies;

  static async injectDB(conn) {
    if (MoviesDAO.movies) {
      return;
    }
    try {
      MoviesDAO.movies = await conn.db(process.env.MOVIEREVIEWS_NS)
        .collection('movies');
    } catch (e) {
      console.error(`unable to connect in MoviesDAO: ${e}`);
    }
  }
}
```

Code Explanation

```
static movies;
```

movies stores the reference to the database.

We then export the class *MoviesDAO* which contains an *async* static method *injectDB*. *injectDB* is called as soon as the server starts and provides the database reference to *movies*.

```
    if (MoviesDAO.movies) {
      return;
    }
```

If the reference already exists, we return.

```
try {
  MoviesDAO.movies = await conn.db(process.env.MOVIEREVIEWS_NS)
    .collection('movies');
}
```

Else, we go ahead to connect to the database name (**process.env.MOVIEREVIEWS_NS**) and *movies* collection.

Lastly, if we fail to get the reference, we send an error message to the console.

```
catch (e) {
  console.error(`unable to connect in MoviesDAO: ${e}`);
}
```

Retrieving Movies

We next define the method to get all movies from the database. Add to *MoviesDAO.js* the below method:

```
static async getMovies({ // default filter
  filters = null,
  page = 0,
  moviesPerPage = 20, // will only get 20 movies at once
} = {}) {
  let query;
  if (filters) {
    if ('title' in filters) {
      query = { $text: { $search: filters.title } };
    } else if ('rated' in filters) {
      query = { rated: { $eq: filters.rated } };
    }
  }

  let cursor;
  try {
    cursor = await MoviesDAO.movies
      .find(query)
      .limit(moviesPerPage)
```

```
            .skip(moviesPerPage * page);
        const moviesList = await cursor.toArray();
        const totalNumMovies = await
MoviesDAO.movies.countDocuments(query);
        return { moviesList, totalNumMovies };
    } catch (e) {
        console.error(`Unable to issue find command, ${e}`);
        return { moviesList: [], totalNumMovies: 0 };
    }
  }
}
```

Code Explanation

```
  static async getMovies({ // default filter
    filters = null,
    page = 0,
    moviesPerPage = 20, // will only get 20 movies at once
  } = {}) {
```

The *getMovies* method accepts a *filter* object as its first argument. The default filter has no filters, retrieves results at page 0 and retrieves 20 movies per page. In our app, we provide filtering results by movie title "title" and movie rating "rated" (e.g. 'G', 'PG,' 'R'). So a *filters* object might look something like:

```
{
  title: "dragon", // search titles with 'dragon' in it
  rated: "G" // search ratings with 'G'
}
```

With the *filters* object, we then construct our query:

```
    if (filters) {
      if ('title' in filters) {
        query = { $text: { $search: filters.title } };
      } else if ('rated' in filters) {
        query = { rated: { $eq: filters.rated } };
      }
    }
```

We have a *query* variable which will be empty unless a user specifies filters in his retrieval, in which case we will put together a query. We first check if the *filters* object contains the property *title* with `if ('title' in filters)`. If so, we use the *$text* query operator together with *$search* to search for movie titles containing the user specified search terms. *$text* also allows us to query using multiple words by separating your words with spaces to query for documents that match any of the search terms (logical OR). E.g. "kill dragon". You can find out more about *$text* at: https://docs.mongodb.com/drivers/node/fundamentals/crud/read-operations/text/ Importantly, we also have to later specify in MongoDB Atlas that we want to enable text searches on the *title* field. We will get to that later.

Queries are very powerful in MongoDB. We have showed the *$text* operator. In the next filter where we check if user has specified the *rated* filter, we check if the user specified value is equal to the value in the database field `query = { rated: { $eq: filters.rated } }`.

```
let cursor;
  try {
    cursor = await MoviesDAO.movies
      .find(query)
      .limit(moviesPerPage)
      .skip(moviesPerPage * page);
    const moviesList = await cursor.toArray();
    const totalNumMovies = await
MoviesDAO.movies.countDocuments(query);
    return { moviesList, totalNumMovies };
  } catch (e) {
    console.error(`Unable to issue find command, ${e}`);
    return { moviesList: [], totalNumMovies: 0 };
  }
}
```

We then find all movies that fit our query and assign it to a *cursor*. If there is any error, we just return an empty *moviesList* and *totalNumMovies* to be 0.

Now, why do we need a cursor? Because our query can potentially match very large sets of documents, a cursor fetches these documents in batches to reduce both memory consumption and network bandwidth usage. Cursors are highly configurable and offer multiple interaction paradigms for different use cases. For example, we used the cursor's *limit* method to cap the number of documents returned as specified in *moviesPerPage*.

Additionally, we use the *skip* method together with *limit*. When *skip* and *limit* is used together, the *skip* applies first and the *limit* only applies to the documents left over after the skip.

This allows us to implement pagination later on in the frontend because we can retrieve a specific page's result. For e.g. if the specific page is 1, we skip 20 results first (`moviesPerPage * 1`) and then retrieve the next 20 results. If the specified page is 2, we skip 40 results (`moviesPerPage * 2`) and then retrieve the next 20 results.

```
const totalNumMovies = await MoviesDAO.movies.countDocuments(query);
```

We then get the total number of movies by counting the number of documents in the query and return *moviesList* and *totalNumMovies* in an object.

Initialising MoviesDAO

In *Index.js*, add the below to import and get the reference to the *MoviesDAO* file.

```
import express from 'express';
import cors from 'cors';
import MoviesRoute from './api/MoviesRoute.js';
import dotenv from 'dotenv';
import mongodb from 'mongodb';
import MoviesDAO from './dao/MoviesDAO.js';
```

Next, add the line below:

```
static async setUpDatabase() {
  ...
  try {
    // Connect to the MongoDB cluster
    await client.connect();
    await MoviesDAO.injectDB(client);
    Index.app.listen(port, () => {
      console.log(`server is running on port:${port}`);
    });
  }
  ...
```

What this does is right after connecting to the database and just before we start the server, we call *injectDB* to get our initial reference to the *movies* collection in the database. In the next chapter, we will create *MoviesController* to access *MoviesDAO*.

CHAPTER 8: CREATING THE MOVIES CONTROLLER

Next, we will create the movies controller that the route file will use to access the *dao* file. In the *api* folder, create a new file *MoviesController.js* with the following code:

```
import MoviesDAO from '../dao/MoviesDAO.js';

export default class MoviesController {
  static async apiGetMovies(req, res, next) {
    const moviesPerPage = req.query.moviesPerPage ?
parseInt(req.query.moviesPerPage) : 20;
    const page = req.query.page ? parseInt(req.query.page) : 0;

    const filters = {};
    if (req.query.rated) {
      filters.rated = req.query.rated;
    } else if (req.query.title) {
      filters.title = req.query.title;
    }

    const { moviesList, totalNumMovies } = await MoviesDAO.getMovies(
      { filters, page, moviesPerPage },
    );

    const response = {
      movies: moviesList,
      page,
      filters,
      entries_per_page: moviesPerPage,
      total_results: totalNumMovies,
    };
    res.json(response);
  }
}
```

Code Explanation

```
import MoviesDAO from '../dao/MoviesDAO.js';
```

We first import the DAO.

```
    static async apiGetMovies(req, res, next) {
    const moviesPerPage = req.query.moviesPerPage ?
parseInt(req.query.moviesPerPage) : 20;
    const page = req.query.page ? parseInt(req.query.page) : 0;
```

When *apiGetMovies* is called via a URL, there will be a query string in the response object *(req.query)* where certain filter parameters might be specified and passed in through key-value pairs. For e.g. we have a URL:

http://localhost:5000/api/v1/movies?title=dragon&moviesPerPage=15&page=0

req.query would return the following JavaScript object after the query string is parsed:

```
{
  title: "dragon",
  moviesPerPage:"15",
  page: "0"
}
```

This is an example of what a query string look like. Later on when we can get our app running, you will get a more complete picture.

One of the query strings is *moviesPerPage*.

```
const moviesPerPage = req.query.moviesPerPage ?
parseInt(req.query.moviesPerPage) : 20;
```

We check if *moviesPerPage* exists, parse it into an integer. We do the same for the *page* query string.

```
    const filters = {};
```

We then start with an empty *filters* object, i.e. no filters are applied at first.

```
if (req.query.rated) {
  filters.rated = req.query.rated;
} else if (req.query.title) {
  filters.title = req.query.title;
}
```

We then check if the *rated* query string exists, then add to the *filters* object. We do the same for *title*.

```
const { moviesList, totalNumMovies } = await MoviesDAO.getMovies(
  { filters, page, moviesPerPage },
);
```

We next call *getMovies* in *MoviesDAO* that we have just implemented. Remember that *getMovies* will return *moviesList* and *totalNumMovies*.

```
const response = {
  movies: moviesList,
  page,
  filters,
  entries_per_page: moviesPerPage,
  total_results: totalNumMovies,
};
res.json(response);
```

We then send a JSON response with the above response object to whoever calls this URL.

Applying the Controller to our Route

Having completed the controller, let's now apply it to our route. Go to *MoviesRoute.js* and add:

```
import MoviesController from './MoviesController.js';

export default class MoviesRoute {
  static configRoutes(router) {
    router.route('/').get(MoviesController.apiGetMovies);
    return router;
  }
}
```

So each time there is a request for URL '/', i.e. *localhost:5000/api/v1/movies/*, we call
MoviesController.apiGetMovies.

Let's test our backend API in the next chapter.

CHAPTER 9: TESTING OUR BACKEND API

Now, let's test if our Node backend server can access the database. Go to the browser and type in the URL http://localhost:5000/api/v1/movies and it should send back movie results (fig. 1).

```
{
    "movies": [
        {
            "_id": "573a1390f29313caabcd4135",
            "plot": "Three men hammer on an anvil and pass a bottle of beer around.",
            "genres": [
                "Short"
            ],
            "runtime": 1,
            "cast": [
                "Charles Kayser",
                "John Ott"
            ],
            "num_mflix_comments": 1,
            "title": "Blacksmith Scene",
            "fullplot": "A stationary camera looks at a large anvil with a blacksmith bel
draws a heated metal rod from the fire, places it on the anvil, and all thre
metal goes back in the fire. One smith pulls out a bottle of beer, and they
the hammering resumes.",
            "countries": [
                "USA"
            ],
            "released": "1893-05-09T00:00:00.000Z",
            "directors": [
                "William K.L. Dickson"
            ],
            "rated": "UNRATED",
            "awards": {
                "wins": 1,
                "nominations": 0,
                "text": "1 win."
            },
```

Figure 1

That means our app has successfully queried the database!

Now, we can test the API in our browser, but it is better to test our API with a tool called Insomnia. Go to https://insomnia.rest/ and download the free Insomnia app (fig. 2).

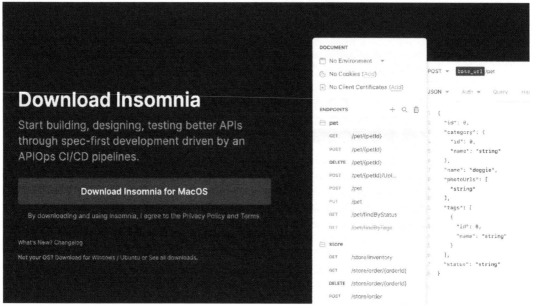

Figure 2

Insomnia helps us test APIs where we can send REST requests to our APIs directly.

Open Insomnia and make a GET request to http://localhost:5000/api/v1/movies (fig. 3).

Figure 3

You should be able to see the retrieved movies on the side (fig. 4).

200 OK | 777 ms | 25.6 KB | 2 Minutes Ago

Preview | Header 8 | Cookie | Timeline

```
{
  "movies": [
    {
      "_id": "573a1390f29313caabcd4135",
      "plot": "Three men hammer on an anvil and pass a bottle of beer around.",
      "genres": [
        "Short"
      ],
      "runtime": 1,
      "cast": [
        "Charles Kayser",
        "John Ott"
      ],
      "num_mflix_comments": 1,
      "title": "Blacksmith Scene",
      "fullplot": "A stationary camera looks at a large anvil with a blacksmith behind it and one on either side. The smith in the middle draws a heated metal rod from the fire, places it on the anvil, and all three begin a rhythmic hammering. After several blows, the metal goes back in the fire. One smith pulls out a bottle of beer, and they each take a swig. Then, out comes the glowing metal and the hammering resumes.",
      "countries": [
        "USA"
      ],
      "released": "1893-05-09T00:00:00.000Z",
      "directors": [
        "William K.L. Dickson"
      ],
      "rated": "UNRATED",
      "awards": {
        "wins": 1,
        "nominations": 0,
        "text": "1 win."
      },
      "lastupdated": "2015-08-26 00:03:50.133000000",
```

Figure 4

You can see the movie's properties like title, plot etc.

```
{
  "movies": [ ↔ 20 ↔ ],
  "page": 0,
  "filters": {},
  "entries_per_page": 20,
  "total_results": 23530
}
```

Figure 5

If you collapse the *movies* array, you can see the *page*, *filters* object, *entries_per_page* and *total_results* property in the response as well (fig. 5). This is because back in *MoviesController.js*, we have defined the response in *getMovies* as:

```
...
const response = {
  movies: moviesList,
  page,
  filters,
  entries_per_page: moviesPerPage,
  total_results: totalNumMovies,
};
res.json(response);
```

The *page, entries_per_page* and *total_results* properties will come in useful later when we implement pagination.

Testing the Filters

Next, let's test the URL with some filters. To apply filters, we add them to the URL query string. For e.g. to filter for movies with rating 'G', we send the following URL in a GET request: http://localhost:5000/api/v1/movies?rated=G and make the request.

You will retrieve movies *rated* 'G'. And at the bottom, we also have the *filters* object, *entries_per_page: 20*, and *total_results: 477* (fig. 6).

```
1 ▾ {
2 ▸   "movies": [ ⇥ 20 ⇤ ],
1349    "page": 0,
1350 ▾  "filters": {
1351      "rated": "G"
1352    },
1353    "entries_per_page": 20,
1354    "total_results": 477
1355  }
```

Figure 6

To filter for page 2, send a GET request to:

http://localhost:5000/api/v1/movies?rated=G&page=2

Search by *title* won't yet work as we have not yet set up the *title* index in MongoDB Atlas. To do so, go to MongoDB Atlas, and in the *sample_mflix* database, *movies* collection, go to 'Indexes' (fig. 7):

48

Figure 7

Select 'Create Index' and under 'Fields', enter:

```
{
  "title": "text",
}
```

COLLECTION
sample_mflix.**movies**

FIELDS
```
1 ▾ {
  2     "title": "text",
  3 }
```

Figure 8

Select 'Confirm' and it will create our index to support text search queries on string content. So if you send a request:

*http://localhost:5000/api/v1/movies?title=**Seven***

It will return movie results with *Seven* in its title.

49

CHAPTER 10: LEAVING MOVIE REVIEWS

Besides searching movies, users can leave reviews for them. So let's create the routes to *post*, *put* and *delete* reviews. *post* is for creating a review, *put* is for editing a review, and *delete* for deleting reviews. In the route file *MoviesRoute.js*, add the routes as shown in **bold**:

```
import MoviesController from './MoviesController.js';
import ReviewsController from './ReviewsController.js';

export default class MoviesRoute {
  static configRoutes(router) {
    router.route('/').get(MoviesController.apiGetMovies);

    router
      .route('/review')
      .post(ReviewsController.apiPostReview)
      .put(ReviewsController.apiUpdateReview)
      .delete(ReviewsController.apiDeleteReview);

    return router;
  }
}
```

Code Explanation

We import the *ReviewsController* which we will create later.

We then add a route '/review' which handles *post*, *put* and *delete* http requests all within this one route call. That is to say, if the '/review' route receives a *post* http request to add a review, we call *apiPostReview*. If '/review' receives a *put* http request to edit a review, call *apiUpdateReview*. And finally, if '/review' receives a *delete* http request to delete a review, call *apiDeleteReview*.

ReviewsController

Next, let's create *ReviewsController.js* with the following code:

```
import ReviewsDAO from '../dao/ReviewsDAO.js';
```

```
export default class ReviewsController {
  static async apiPostReview(req, res, next) {
    try {
      const movieId = req.body.movie_id;
      const { review } = req.body;
      const userInfo = {
        name: req.body.name,
        _id: req.body.user_id,
      };

      const date = new Date();

      const ReviewResponse = await ReviewsDAO.addReview(
        movieId,
        userInfo,
        review,
        date,
      );
      res.json({ status: 'success ' });
    } catch (e) {
      res.status(500).json({ error: e.message });
    }
  }
}
```

Code Explanation

```
import ReviewsDAO from '../dao/ReviewsDAO.js';
```

We first import *ReviewsDAO* which we will create later. We then have the *apiPostReview* method:

```
const movieId = req.body.movie_id;
const { review } = req.body;
const userInfo = {
  name: req.body.name,
  _id: req.body.user_id,
};
```

We get information from the request's *body* parameter. Previously in *MoviesController*, we got information from the request's query parameter as we extracted data from the URL e.g. *req.query.title*. This time, we retrieve the data from the body of the request. In the Angular frontend of the app (which we will implement later), we call this endpoint with something like:

```
this._http.post<any>("http:// localhost:5000/api/v1/movies/review", data)
```

The *data* object generated in the frontend will look something like:

```
{
    review: "great movie",
    name: "john",
    user_id: "123",
    movie_id: "573a1390f29313caabcd6223"
}
```

data will be passed in as the request's body. Thus, to retrieve each of the field values, we use *req.body.movie_id*, *req.body.review* etc.

```
const ReviewResponse = await ReviewsDAO.addReview(
    movieId,
    userInfo,
    review,
    date,
);
```

We send the information to *ReviewsDAO.addReview* which we will create later.

```
...
res.json({ status: 'success ' });
} catch (e) {
    res.status(500).json({ error: e.message });
}
```

Finally, we return 'success' if the post works and an error if it didn't.

ReviewsController *apiUpdateView*

We next create the *apiUpdateReview* method which is quite similar to the *apiPostReview* method:

```
static async apiUpdateReview(req, res, next) {
  try {
    const reviewId = req.body.review_id;
    const { review } = req.body;

    const date = new Date();

    const ReviewResponse = await ReviewsDAO.updateReview(
      reviewId,
      req.body.user_id,
      review,
      date,
    );

    const { error } = ReviewResponse;
    if (error) {
      res.status.json({ error });
    }

    if (ReviewResponse.modifiedCount === 0) {
      throw new Error('unable to update review. User may not be
original poster');
    }
    res.json({ status: 'success ' });
  } catch (e) {
    res.status(500).json({ error: e.message });
  }
}
```

Code Explanation

Like *apiPostReview*, *apiUpdateReview* will be called by the frontend with a request like the below:

```
axios.put("https://localhost:5000/api/v1/movies/review", data);
```

We extract the *movieId* and *review* text similar to what we have done in posting a review.

```
  const ReviewResponse = await ReviewsDAO.updateReview(
    reviewId,
    req.body.user_id,
    review,
    date,
  );
```

We then call *ReviewsDAO.updateReview* and pass in *user_id* to ensure that the user who is updating the view is the one who has created it.

```
if (ReviewResponse.modifiedCount === 0) {
    throw new Error('unable to update review. User may not be
original poster');
    }
```

updateReview returns a document *ReviewResponse* which contains the property *modifiedCount*. *modifiedCount* contains the number of modified documents. We check *modifiedCount* to ensure that it is not zero. If it is, it means the review has not been updated and we throw an error.

ReviewsController *apiDeleteView*

We lastly have *apiDeleteReview*:

```
static async apiDeleteReview(req, res, next) {
  try {
    const reviewId = req.body.review_id;
    const userId = req.body.user_id;
    console.log('apiDeleteReview', req.body);
    const ReviewResponse = await ReviewsDAO.deleteReview(
      reviewId,
      userId,
    );

    res.json({ status: 'success ' });
  } catch (e) {
    res.status(500).json({ error: e.message });
  }
}
```

Like *apiPostReview* and *apiUpdateReview*, we extract *reviewId* and *userId*. With *userId*, we ensure that the user deleting the view is the one who has created the view. Now, let's create *ReviewsDAO*.

ReviewsDAO

In *dao* folder, create the file *ReviewsDAO.js* with the following code:

```
import mongodb from 'mongodb';

export default class ReviewsDAO {
  static reviews;

  static ObjectId = mongodb.ObjectId;

  static async injectDB(conn) {
    if (ReviewsDAO.reviews) {
      return;
    }
    try {
      ReviewsDAO.reviews = await
conn.db(process.env.MOVIEREVIEWS_NS).collection('reviews');
    } catch (e) {
      console.error(`unable to establish connection handle in reviewDAO:
${e}`);
    }
  }
}
```

Code Explanation

```
import mongodb from 'mongodb';
static ObjectId = mongodb.ObjectId;
```

We import *mongodb* to get access to *ObjectId*. We need *ObjectId* to convert an id string to a MongoDB Object id later on.

```
  if (ReviewsDAO.reviews) {
    return;
  }
  try {
    ReviewsDAO.reviews = await
conn.db(process.env.MOVIEREVIEWS_NS).collection('reviews');
  }
```

For the rest of the code, notice that it is similar to *MoviesDAO*. If *ReviewsDAO.reviews* is not filled, we then access the database *reviews* collection. Note that if the *reviews* collection doesn't yet exist in the database, MongoDB automatically creates it for us.

Initiating ReviewsDAO in Index.js

We will also need to initiate *ReviewsDAO* as we did for *MoviesDAO* in *Index.js*. In *Index.js*, add in the below two lines:

```
import express from 'express';
import cors from 'cors';
import MoviesRoute from './api/MoviesRoute.js';
import dotenv from 'dotenv';
import mongodb from 'mongodb';
import MoviesDAO from './dao/MoviesDAO.js';
import ReviewsDAO from './dao/ReviewsDAO.js';
...

  static async setUpDatabase() {
    ...
    try {
      // Connect to the MongoDB cluster
      await client.connect();
      await MoviesDAO.injectDB(client);
      await ReviewsDAO.injectDB(client);
      Index.app.listen(port, () => {
        console.log(`server is running on port:${port}`);
      });
    }
    ...
```

ReviewsDAO addReview

In *ReviewsDAO.js*, add in the *addReview* method for creating a review:

```
static async addReview(movieId, user, review, date) {
  try {
    const reviewDoc = {
      name: user.name,
      user_id: user._id,
      date,
      review,
      movie_id: ReviewsDAO.ObjectId(movieId),
    };
    return await ReviewsDAO.reviews.insertOne(reviewDoc);
  } catch (e) {
    console.error(`unable to post review: ${e}`);
    return { error: e };
  }
}
```

We first create a *reviewDoc* document object. Note that for the *movie_id*, we have to first convert the *movieId* string to a MongoDB object id. We then insert it into the *reviews* collection with *insertOne*.

ReviewsDAO updateReview

In *ReviewsDAO.js*, add in the below *updateReview* method for editing a review:

```
static async updateReview(reviewId, userId, review, date) {
  try {
    const updateResponse = await ReviewsDAO.reviews.updateOne(
      { user_id: userId, _id: ReviewsDAO.ObjectId(reviewId) },
      { $set: { review, date } },
    );
    return updateResponse;
  } catch (e) {
    console.error(`unable to update review: ${e}`);
    return { error: e };
  }
}
```

When calling *reviews.updateOne*, we specify the first argument `{ user_id: userId, _id:` `ReviewsDAO.ObjectId(reviewId) }` to filter for an existing review created by *userId* and with *reviewId*. If the review exists, we then update it with the second argument which contains the new review text and date.

ReviewsDAO deleteReview

In *ReviewsDAO.js*, add in the below *deleteReview* method for deleting a review:

```
static async deleteReview(reviewId, userId) {
  try {
    const deleteResponse = await ReviewsDAO.reviews.deleteOne({
      _id: ReviewsDAO.ObjectId(reviewId),
      user_id: userId,
    });
    return deleteResponse;
  } catch (e) {
    console.error(`unable to delete review: ${e}`);
    return { error: e };
  }
}
```

When calling *reviews.deleteOne*, similar to *updateOne*, we specify `ReviewsDAO.ObjectId(reviewId)` to look for an existing review with *reviewId* and created by *userId*. If the review exists, we then delete it.

CHAPTER 11: TESTING THE REVIEWS API

To test the reviews API, first get an existing movie id. You can just send a *get* request to http://localhost:5000/api/v1/movies to retrieve all movies and then pick any movie id.

Next, make a *post* request to: *localhost:5000/api/v1/movies/review* and provide a review body something like:

```
{
  "movie_id": "573a1390f29313caabcd4135",
  "review": "great movie",
  "user_id": "1234",
  "name": "john"
}
```

Figure 1

*Note: Make sure that *movie_id* is in a valid *ObjectID* format. Else, MongoDB will not accept it and will throw an error something like:

```
"Error: Argument passed in must be a single String of 12 bytes or a
string of 24 hex characters"
```

Click 'Send' and you should get a *status: success* response. And if you go to MongoDB Atlas, your newly posted review should be in the *reviews* collection.

Testing Edit

Now let's see if we can edit a review. We will need the *review_id* of an existing review. With the *review_id*, send a *put* request in Insomnia to *localhost:5000/api/v1/movies/review* with a JSON object like:

```
{
  "review_id": "60987656387806c22051bb67",
  "review": "bad movie",
  "user_id": "1234",
  "name": "john"
}
```

And if you go to MongoDB Atlas (you might need to refresh it), the review should be edited.

Testing Delete

Now, let's test the *delete* review endpoint. Send a *delete* request to *localhost:5000/api/v1/movies/review* with a JSON object like:

```
{
  "review_id": "609879ea2c7565c289746500",
  "user_id": "1234"
}
```

And if you go to MongoDB Atlas and select refresh, the review will no longer exist.

So, we have tested our add, edit and delete review API endpoints!

CHAPTER 12: ROUTE TO GET A SINGLE MOVIE AND ITS RATINGS

We are getting close to completing the back end. We just need to add two more routes, a route to get a specific movie (with its reviews) and a route to get all ratings. In the *MoviesRoute.js* route file, add the two routes as shown:

```
...
router.route('/').get(MoviesController.apiGetMovies);
router.route('/id/:id').get(MoviesController.apiGetMovieById);
router.route('/ratings').get(MoviesController.apiGetRatings);
...
```

Code Explanation

```
router.route('/id/:id').get(MoviesController.apiGetMovieById);
```

This route retrieves a specific movie and all reviews associated for that movie.

```
router.route('/ratings').get(MoviesController.apiGetRatings);
```

This route returns us a list of movie ratings (e.g. 'G', 'PG', 'R') so that a user can select the ratings from a dropdown menu in the front end.

MoviesController.js

Next, let's implement the *apiGetMovieById* and *apiGetRatings* methods in *MoviesController*. Add in the following two methods into *MoviesController.js*:

```
import MoviesDAO from '../dao/MoviesDAO.js';

export default class MoviesController {
  ...
  static async apiGetMovieById(req, res, next) {
    try {
      const id = req.params.id || {};
      const movie = await MoviesDAO.getMovieById(id);
```

```
    if (!movie) {
      res.status(404).json({ error: 'not found' });
      return;
    }
    res.json(movie);
  } catch (e) {
    console.log(`api, ${e}`);
    res.status(500).json({ error: e });
  }
}

static async apiGetRatings(req, res, next) {
  try {
    const propertyTypes = await MoviesDAO.getRatings();
    res.json(propertyTypes);
  } catch (e) {
    console.log(`api,${e}`);
    res.status(500).json({ error: e });
  }
}
}
}
```

Code Explanation

```
    const id = req.params.id || {};
```

We first look for an *id* parameter which is the value after the '/' in a URL. E.g.
localhost:5000/api/v1/movies/id/12345

Note the difference between a request query and parameter. In a query, there is a '?' after the URL followed by a key-value e.g. /api/v1/movies?title=dragon
In a parameter, it's the value after '/'.

```
    const movie = await MoviesDAO.getMovieById(id);
    if (!movie) {
      res.status(404).json({ error: 'not found' });
      return;
    }
    res.json(movie);
```

We then call *MoviesDAO.getMovieById* which we will create later. The method returns us the specific movie in a JSON response. If there is no movie, we return an error.

The *apiGetRatings* is more straightforward. We do not have to feed in any parameters, but simply call *MoviesDAO.apiGetRatings*.

Implementing *getMovieById* and *getRatings* in *MoviesDAO*

We will first implement *getRatings* in *MoviesDAO.js* as it is more straightforward. Add the below method into *MoviesDAO*:

```
static async getRatings() {
  let ratings = [];
  try {
    ratings = await MoviesDAO.movies.distinct('rated');
    return ratings;
  } catch (e) {
    console.error('unable to get ratings, $(e)');
    return ratings;
  }
}
```

We use *MoviesDAO.movies.distinct* to get all the distinct *rated* values from the *movies* collection. We then assign the results to the *ratings* array.

getMovieById

Next, let's implement *getMovieById* which can be a little complicated because other than getting the specific movie from the *movies* collection, we will also be getting its related reviews from the *reviews* collection.

Add the below method, the import statement, and the static attribute in **bold** into *MoviesDAO*:

```
import mongodb from 'mongodb';

export default class MoviesDAO{
  static movies;

  static ObjectId = mongodb.ObjectId;
```

```
...
static async getMovieById(id) {
  try {
    return await MoviesDAO.movies.aggregate([
      {
        $match: {
          _id: new MoviesDAO.ObjectId(id),
        },
      },
      {
        $lookup:
        {
          from: 'reviews',
          localField: '_id',
          foreignField: 'movie_id',
          as: 'reviews',
        },
      },
    ]).next();
  } catch (e) {
    console.error(`something went wrong in getMovieById: ${e}`);
    throw e;
  }
}
...
```

Code Explanation

We use *aggregate* to provide a sequence of data aggregation operations. In our case, the first operation is *$match*, where we look for the movie document that matches the specified id.

Next, we use the *$lookup* operator to perform an equality join using the *_id* field from the *movie* document with the *movie_id* field from *reviews* collection.

The *$lookup* stage has the following syntax:

```
{
    $lookup:
      {
        from: <collection to join>,
        localField: <field from the input document>,
        foreignField: <field from the documents of the "from" collection>,
        as: <output array field>
      }
}
```

This finds all the reviews with the specific movie id and returns the specific movie together with the reviews in an array.

$lookup is just one component of the MongoDB aggregation framework. MongoDB aggregations are very powerful but we will just touch a small part of this now.

Testing our App

Now, let's test the two routes we have added into *MoviesRoute.js*:

```
router.route('/id/:id').get(MoviesController.apiGetMovieById);
router.route('/ratings').get(MoviesController.apiGetRatings);
```

Let's first test the */ratings* route. Send a *GET* request to: *localhost:5000/api/v1/movies/ratings/*. You should get all the ratings returned:

```
[
    "AO",
    "APPROVED",
    "Approved",
    "G",
    "GP",
    "M",
    "NC-17",
    "NOT RATED",
    "Not Rated",
    "OPEN",
    "PASSED",
    "PG",
    "PG-13",
```

```
    "R",
    "TV-14",
    "TV-G",
    "TV-MA",
    "TV-PG",
    "TV-Y7",
    "UNRATED",
    "X"
]
```

We will later use this to populate the dropdown menu.

Testing our app – Get Specific Movie

Next, let's test the */id/:id* route. Send a GET request to:

`localhost:5000/api/v1/movies/id/573a1390f29313caabcd6223`
(fill in your own movie id)

and you should get the specific movie data and the *reviews* array in the response too.

```
{
    "_id": "573a1390f29313caabcd6223",
    "plot": "..",
    "genres": [
        "Comedy",
        "Drama",
        "Family"
    ],
    "runtime": 65,
    "cast": [
        "Mary Pickford",
        "Madlaine Traverse",
        "Charles Wellesley",
        "Gladys Fairbanks"
    ],
    "title": "The Poor Little Rich Girl",
        ...
```

```
  "reviews": [
    {
      "_id": "6098bdd132398dc6576a89a8",
      "name": "jason",
      "user_id": "1234",
      "date": "2021-05-10T05:00:01.675Z",
      "review": "nice!",
      "movie_id": "573a1390f29313caabcd6223"
    },
    {
      "_id": "6098bddf32398dc6576a89a9",
      "name": "john",
      "user_id": "1236",
      "date": "2021-05-10T05:00:15.380Z",
      "review": "bad!",
      "movie_id": "573a1390f29313caabcd6223"
    }
  ]
}
```

If the *reviews* array is empty, create some reviews for the movie first by sending POST requests to *localhost:5000/api/v1/movies/review/* and JSON objects to add the reviews e.g.

```
{
  "movie_id":"573a1390f29313caabcd6223",
  "review":"nice!",
  "user_id":"1234",
  "name":"jason",
}
```

```
{
  "movie_id":"573a1390f29313caabcd6223",
  "review":"bad!",
  "user_id":"1236",
  "name":"john"
}
```

Send the GET request to get the specific movie again and you should get *reviews* populated in the response.

And that completes our backend implemented with Node and Express. All our routes work. So let's create our frontend and then connect it to our backend.

ANGULAR FRONTEND

CHAPTER 13: INTRODUCTION TO ANGULAR

For those who have some experience with Angular, this section will be familiar to you. But even if you are new to Angular, you should still be able to follow along. If you are interested in digging into Angular details, you can check out my Angular book.

Before we go on further, let's explain briefly what is Angular. Angular is a framework maintained by Google for creating single-page client applications with components. For example, if we want to build a storefront module like what we see on Amazon, we can divide it into three components. The search bar component, sidebar component and products component (fig. 1).

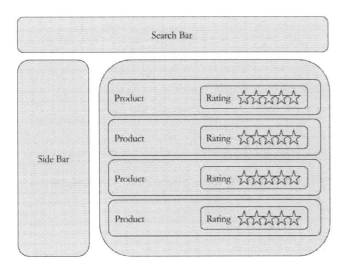

Figure 1

Components can also contain other components. For example, in *products* component where we display a list of products, we do so using multiple *product* components. Also, in each *product* component, we can have a *rating* component.

The benefit of such an architecture helps us to break up a large application into smaller manageable components. Plus, we can reuse components within the application or even in a different application. For example, we can reuse the rating component in a different application.

An Angular component consists of a HTML template and a component class that has its own data and logic to control the HTML template. When the values of its data change, Angular will update the concerned UI component.

Below is an example of a Product component with a 'rating' property.

```
export class ProductComponent {

  rating: number = 0;
  setRating(value){

    ...

  }
}
```

A component is simply a plain TypeScript class like any other class that has properties and methods. The properties hold the data for the view and the methods implement the behavior of a view, like what should happen if I click a button.

Modules

An Angular app is made up of separate modules which consist of closely related components of functionality. When we first begin creating our app, we will have only one module, the root module *AppModule*. For small applications, the root module may be the only module. But most apps have multiple feature modules, each being groups of components that perform a role. For example, a social media app will have a Post module, Message module, Followers module and so on.

Installing Angular CLI

The Angular CLI is a *Command Line Interface* tool that makes creating an Angular project, adding files, and other ongoing development tasks like testing, bundling and deployment easier.

To install Angular CLI from the command line, type

```
npm install -g @angular/cli
```

Creating a New Project with Angular CLI

First, let's go to our *movie-reviews* directory. In it, we will create our initial Angular project by running the CLI command 'ng new' and provide the project name:

```
ng new <project name>
```

In our case, our project will be called *frontend*. So run the command:

```
ng new frontend
```

You will then be asked a question, "Would you like to add Angular routing?". Answer 'y'.

Angular routing routes different URLs to different pages in our app. It interprets a browser URL as an instruction to navigate to various components. We can bind the router to links on a page and it will navigate to the appropriate application view when the user clicks a link.

In the next question, "Which stylesheet format would you like to use?", just select 'CSS'.

For the rest of the questions, just press 'Enter' to give the default answers for now. Angular CLI will then create your project folder and install the necessary Angular *npm* packages and other dependencies to create your Angular application. Note that this takes a few minutes.

When the folder is created, navigate to it by typing.

```
cd frontend
```

Next, type

```
ng serve --open
```

The *ng serve* command launches the server, watches your files and rebuilds the app as you make changes to those files. The *--open* (or just -o) option automatically opens your browser to http://localhost:4200/. If your installation and setup was successful, you should see your app greet you with the page as shown in fig. 1.

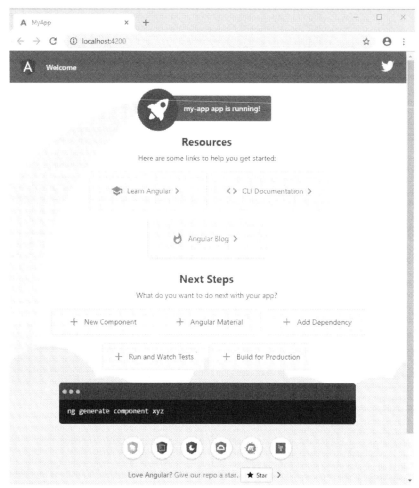

Figure 1

Project File Review

Now let's look at the project files created for us. When you open the *movie-reviews/frontend* project folder in VScode editor, you will find a couple of files (fig. 2).

fig. 2

We will not go through all the files as our focus is to get started with our Angular app quickly. But we will briefly go through some important files and folders.

Our app lives in the *src* folder. All Angular components, templates, styles, images and anything else our app needs go here. Other files outside of this folder are meant to support building your app. In the course of this book, you will come to appreciate the uses for the rest of the files and folders.

In the *src* folder, we have *main.ts* which is the main entry point for our app. It compiles the application with the JIT compiler and bootstraps the application's root module *AppModule* to run in the browser.

tsconfig.json is the Typescript compiler configuration for our app. i.e., how to compile our TypeScript files into Javascript.

package.json is the node package configuration which lists the third-party packages our project uses. You can also add custom scripts here.

node_modules folder is created by Node.js and puts all third-party modules listed in *package.json* in it.

In the *app* folder, we find a couple of other TypeScript files:

app.module.ts is the root module that tells Angular how to assemble our application. As mentioned earlier, an Angular app comprises of separate modules which are closely related blocks of functionality. Every Angular application has at least one module: the root module, named *AppModule* here. For many small applications, the root module *AppModule* alone is enough. For bigger modules, we can create multiple modules. You can read more about modules in my <u>Angular book</u>.

```
import { NgModule } from '@angular/core';
import { BrowserModule } from '@angular/platform-browser';

import { AppRoutingModule } from './app-routing.module';
import { AppComponent } from './app.component';

@NgModule({
  declarations: [
    AppComponent
  ],
  imports: [
    BrowserModule,
    AppRoutingModule
  ],
  providers: [],
  bootstrap: [AppComponent]
})
export class AppModule { }
```

A module is a class with the *@NgModule* decorator. Angular has decorators that attach metadata to classes so that it knows what those classes are and how they should work. For example, modules and components have decorators that tell Angular that they are modules and components respectively. The *@NgModule* decorator is a function that takes a single metadata object whose properties describe the module. The most important properties are:

declarations - to declare which components, directives or pipes belong to this module. For now, it is just *AppComponent*. But we will soon start adding other components to this array.

imports - to specify what other modules whose exported classes are needed by components declared in this module. Angular comes with pre-defined modules like the *BrowserModule*. As a brief introduction, the *BrowserModule* contains browser-related functionality. It also contains the *common* module which has *ngIf* and *ngFor* which we will introduce later.

Since our application is a web application that runs in a browser, the root module needs to import the *BrowserModule* from *@angular/platform-browser* to the *imports* array. For now, our app doesn't do anything else, so you don't need any other modules. In a real application, you'd likely import other commonly used modules like *FormsModule* and *HttpClientModule* which we will introduce later.

providers - to specify any application wide services we want to use

app.component.ts

```
import { Component } from '@angular/core';

@Component({
  selector: 'app-root',
  templateUrl: './app.component.html',
  styleUrls: ['./app.component.css']
})
export class AppComponent {
  title = 'frontend';
}
```

Every Angular application has at least one component: the root component named *AppComponent* in *app.component.ts*. Components are the basic building blocks of Angular applications. A component controls a portion of the screen, a view - through its associated HTML template, *app.component.html. app.component.css* is the CSS file referenced from *app.component.ts.*

Note: You will notice that there is also a *app.component.spec.ts* file. This file allows you to unit test your app with other testing libraries. We will not be covering Unit Testing as it is beyond the scope of this book.

We define our component's application logic (what it does to support the view) inside a class. The class interacts with the view through properties and methods. For now, our root app component class has only a variable `title`.

This class is decorated with the Component decorator *@Component*. Like the module decorator, the component decorator adds metadata above this class. Because decorators are functions, we need to use the prefix @ sign to call the *@Component* function with its brackets *@Component(...)*. All components in Angular are essentially decorated TypeScript classes.

```
@Component({
  selector: 'app-root',
  templateUrl: './app.component.html',
  styleUrls: ['./app.component.css']
})
```

Add Bootstrap framework:

We will use *Bootstrap* to make our UI look more professional. Bootstrap (https://getbootstrap.com – fig. 2) is a library of reusable frontend components that contain HTML and CSS based templates to help build user interface components (like forms, buttons, icons) for web applications.

Build fast, responsive sites with Bootstrap

Quickly design and customize responsive mobile-first sites with Bootstrap, the world's most popular front-end open source toolkit, featuring Sass variables and mixins, responsive grid system, extensive prebuilt components, and powerful JavaScript plugins.

Get started   Download

Currently **v5.0.2** · v4.6.x docs · All releases

Figure 2

To get started with Bootstrap, we need to reference *bootstrap.css* in our *index.html*. Go to *getbootstrap.com* and under 'Getting Started', copy the *bootstrap.min.css* stylesheet link (fig. 3).

CSS

Copy-paste the stylesheet `<link>` into your `<head>` before all other stylesheets to load our CSS.

```
<link href="https://cdn.jsdelivr.net/npm/bootstrap@5.0.2/dist/css/bootstrap.min.css
```
Copy

Figure 3 - Note: as of book's writing, version of Bootstrap is v5.1.0.

Paste the link into your *<head>* of *index.html* as shown below in **bold**.

```
<!doctype html>
<html lang="en">
<head>
  <meta charset="utf-8">
  <title>Frontend</title>
  <base href="/">
  <meta name="viewport" content="width=device-width, initial-scale=1">
  <link rel="icon" type="image/x-icon" href="favicon.ico">
  <link
href="https://cdn.jsdelivr.net/npm/bootstrap@5.0.2/dist/css/bootstrap.min
.css" rel="stylesheet" integrity="…" crossorigin="anonymous">
</head>
```

```
<body>
  <app-root></app-root>
</body>
</html>
```

Test our App

Now, let's make sure that everything is working so far. Delete all the existing HTML in *app.component.html* and fill it with the below *Alert* component markup (taken from *https://getbootstrap.com/docs/5.0/components/alerts/*):

```
<div class="alert alert-primary" role="alert">
  A simple primary alert—check it out!
</div>
```

To test run our app, go to the *frontend* directory in the Terminal and run:

```
ng serve --open
```

It will then open up *localhost:4200* in your browser and render the Alert Component (fig. 3).

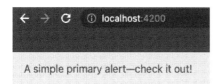

Figure 3

So our Angular app's running well with Bootstrap! In the next chapter, we will create a navigation header bar.

CHAPTER 14: CREATE NAVIGATION HEADER BAR

Let's add a navigation header bar which allows a user to select different routes to access different components in the main part of the page. We will start by creating some simple components and our router will load the different components depending on the URL route a user selects.

Let's first create a *components* folder in *src/app* (fig. 1).

Figure 1

Go to the *components* folder in the Terminal where we will create four new components with the Angular CLI:
- *MoviesList* component to list movies
- *Movie* component to list a single movie
- *AddReview* component to add a review
- *Login* component

To generate the *MoviesList* component, enter the following command:

```
ng generate component movies-list
```

Alternatively, you can use the shortcut:

```
ng g c movies-list
```

The command creates a directory *src/app/components/movies-list* with four files:
- *movies-list.component.ts* (TypeScript file with a component class named *MoviesListComponent*)
- *movies-list.component.html* (HTML file for the component template)

- *movies-list.component.css* (*css* file for the component styles)
- *movies-list.component.spec.ts* (a test file for the *MoviesListComponent* class)

The *ng generate component* command also adds the *MoviesListComponent* as a declaration in the *@NgModule* decorator of the *src/app/app.module.ts* file:

```
@NgModule({
  declarations: [
    AppComponent,
    MoviesListComponent
  ],
...
```

We shall revisit this later. Let's look at the *movies-list.component.html* and *movies-list.component.ts* files:

movies-list.component.html

```
<p>movies-list works!</p>
```

movies-list.component.html simply displays a message which is enough for now as we just need boilerplate code for our four components.

movies-list.component.ts

```
import { Component, OnInit } from '@angular/core';

@Component({
  selector: 'app-movies-list',
  templateUrl: './movies-list.component.html',
  styleUrls: ['./movies-list.component.css']
})
export class MoviesListComponent implements OnInit {

  constructor() { }

  ngOnInit(): void {
  }
}
```

We similarly have an auto-generated boilerplate *MoviesList* component class.

Let's continue generating the other components' boilerplate code by running the commands:

84

```
ng g c movie
ng g c add-review
ng g c login
```

We will later revisit the above components and implement them in greater detail.

app.module.ts

In *app.module.ts*, note that the components we have just generated are automatically imported and added:

```
import { NgModule } from '@angular/core';
import { BrowserModule } from '@angular/platform-browser';

import { AppRoutingModule } from './app-routing.module';
import { AppComponent } from './app.component';
import { MoviesListComponent } from './components/movies-list/movies-
list.component';
import { MovieComponent } from './components/movie/movie.component';
import { AddReviewComponent } from './components/add-review/add-
review.component';
import { LoginComponent } from './components/login/login.component';

@NgModule({
  declarations: [
    AppComponent,
    MoviesListComponent,
    MovieComponent,
    AddReviewComponent,
    LoginComponent
  ],
  imports: [
    BrowserModule,
    AppRoutingModule,
  ],
  providers: [],
  bootstrap: [AppComponent]
})
export class AppModule { }
```

Navbar Component

Bootstrap has different components that you can use. To use a component, go to the Bootstrap documentation (*getbootstrap.com*), copy the component's markup and edit it for your own purposes.

We will grab a navbar component from Bootstrap
(https://getbootstrap.com/docs/5.0/components/navbar/ - fig. 2)

Figure 2

Copy and paste the *Navbar* markup into *app.component.html*. Let's remove the *Dropdown* and *Search* form elements from the *Navbar* for simplicity. Your *app.component.html* should now look something like:

```
<nav class="navbar navbar-expand-lg navbar-light bg-light">
  <div class="container-fluid">
    <a class="navbar-brand" href="#">Navbar</a>
    <button class="navbar-toggler" type="button">
      <span class="navbar-toggler-icon"></span>
    </button>
    <div class="collapse navbar-collapse">
      <ul class="navbar-nav me-auto mb-2 mb-lg-0">
        <li class="nav-item">
          <a class="nav-link active" aria-current="page" href="#">Home</a>
        </li>
        <li class="nav-item">
          <a class="nav-link" href="#">Link</a>
        </li>
      </ul>
    </div>
  </div>
</nav>
```

We now have a basic bootstrap navbar. If you run the app now, it should give you something like in figure 3:

Navbar Home Link

Figure 3

In the current navbar, we have three links. The first is 'Navbar' which is like the brand of the website. Sometimes, this would be a logo, image, or just some text. We will leave it as a text.

The other two are 'Home' and 'Link'. We will change 'Home' to 'Movies' and 'Link' with 'Login'. We will later implement that it shows 'Login' or 'Logout' depending on the user's login state.

So make the following changes in **bold**:

```
<nav class="navbar navbar-expand-lg navbar-light bg-light">
  <div class="container-fluid">
    <a class="navbar-brand" routerLink="movies">Movies Reviews</a>
    <button class="navbar-toggler" type="button">
      <span class="navbar-toggler-icon"></span>
    </button>
    <div class="collapse navbar-collapse">
      <ul class="navbar-nav me-auto mb-2 mb-lg-0">
        <li class="nav-item">
          <a class="nav-link active" routerLink="movies">Movies</a>
        </li>
        <li class="nav-item">
          <a class="nav-link" routerLink="login">Login</a>
        </li>
      </ul>
    </div>
  </div>
</nav>
```

Code Explanation

```
<a class="navbar-brand" routerLink="movies">Movies Reviews</a>
...
<a class="nav-link" routerLink="login">Login</a>
```

We use the *routerLink* directive (not *href*) to route to the target route specified. For e.g., when a user clicks on 'Movies', it will route to the *MoviesList* component. The actual route definitions will be declared and explained in the next chapter.

CHAPTER 15: DEFINING OUR ROUTES

To enable routing between components, we need to define our routes. We define our routes in the *app-routing.module.ts* file. *app-routing.module.ts* should already be generated because we answered 'y' to the question "Do you want to use routing" when we created our Angular project. (even if we answered 'n', we can still manually create and add *app-routing.module.ts* to our project).

In *app-routing.module.ts*, import the components and add the *routes array* with the below codes in **bold**:

```
import { NgModule } from '@angular/core';
import { RouterModule, Routes } from '@angular/router';
import { MoviesListComponent } from './components/movies-list/movies-list.component';
import { MovieComponent } from './components/movie/movie.component';
import { AddReviewComponent } from './components/add-review/add-review.component';
import { LoginComponent } from './components/login/login.component';

const routes: Routes = [
  {
    path: '',
    component: MoviesListComponent,
  },
  {
    path: 'movies',
    component: MoviesListComponent,
  },
  {
    path: 'movies/review/:id',
    component: AddReviewComponent,
  },
  {
    path: 'movies/:id',
    component: MovieComponent,
  },
  {
    path: 'login',
    component: LoginComponent,
  },
```

```
];

@NgModule({
  imports: [RouterModule.forRoot(routes)],
  exports: [RouterModule]
})
export class AppRoutingModule { }
```

Code Explanation

app.routing.ts contains our route definitions.

```
import { RouterModule, Routes } from '@angular/router';
```

We import *Routes* and *RouterModule* from Router library which provide the essential routing functionalities.

```
const routes: Routes = [
  {
    path: '',
    component: MoviesListComponent,
  },
  {
    path: 'movies',
    component: MoviesListComponent,
  },
  ...
]
```

We then define an array of *Routes* definition object called *routes*. Each route definition has at least two properties, *path* which is the unique name we assign to our route and *component* which specifies the associated component.

In our route definition, we specify our four components, *MoviesListComponent*, *AddReviewComponent*, *MovieComponent* and *LoginComponent*.

Our route definition tells Angular that:
-   if the path changes to '/', or '/movies', Angular should create an instance of *MoviesListComponent* and render it in the DOM. E.g.:
    ```
    <a class="nav-link active" routerLink="movies">Movies</a>
    ```
-   if the path changes to '/login', Angular should create an instance of *LoginComponent* and render

it in the DOM. E.g.:

```
<a class="nav-link" routerLink="login">Login</a>
```

- If the path changes to 'movies/:id', Angular should create an instance of MovieComponent and render it in the DOM. This is a route that takes in route parameters. Why do we need this? Say from the *MoviesList* page, we want to navigate to the page of a specific movie, we pass in the movie id via route parameters. '/:id' represents the id route parameter. With this route, we navigate to a specific movie's URL

  e.g.: http://localhost:4200/movies/3498324. Angular will render the *MovieComponent* with the parameter id '3498324'.

- '/movies/review/:id' is the route to render the *AddReview* component for a particular movie.

```
@NgModule({
  imports: [RouterModule.forRoot(routes)],
  exports: [RouterModule]
})
```

We pass in the *routes* array into the *forRoot* method of *RouterModule*. *forRoot* returns a module object which we provide to *imports*.

```
export class AppRoutingModule { }
```

We export *AppRoutingModule* so that we can import it in *AppModule*. Note that *routes* array is declared as a *const* which is a good practice so that no one will modify our routes making our application more reliable.

Router Outlet

To specify where we want Angular to render our requested component when the user clicks on a *routerLink*, we specify *<router-outlet></router-outlet>* in the DOM. In our case, we want to render the component below the navbar. So in *app.component.html*, we add *router-outlet* to the template (below *<nav>*):

```
<nav class="navbar navbar-expand-lg navbar-light bg-light">
  ...
</nav>
<div class="container mt-3">
  <router-outlet></router-outlet>
</div>
```

Testing our Routes

If you run your Angular frontend now and click on the different links in the navbar, you will see the different components being rendered (fig. 1).

Figure 1

CHAPTER 16: DEFINING INTERFACES

Before we attempt to retrieve the list of movies from the backend server, we define interfaces to hold the data received from the API. We represent an *Interface* by a simple class that contains properties. In *src/app/*, create a new folder called *interfaces*.

Create a new *user.ts* file inside the *interfaces* folder with the following content:

```
export default interface User{
    name: string;
    id: string;
}
```

Create a new *movie.ts* file inside the *interfaces* folder with the following content:

```
import Review from 'src/app/interfaces/review';

export default interface Movie{
    poster: string;
    title: string;
    rated: string;
    plot: string;
    _id: string;
    reviews: Array<Review>;
}
```

Create a new *movies.ts* file inside the *interfaces* folder with the following content:

```
import Movie from 'src/app/interfaces/movie';

export default interface Movies{
    movies: Array<Movie>;
}
```

Create a new *review.ts* file inside the *interfaces* folder with the following content:

```
export default interface Review{
    name: string;
    date: Date;
    review: string;
    user_id: string;
```

```
    _id: string
}
```

Note that the property names in the interfaces map to the exact property names received from the backend API. With interfaces, we enforce the structure of the data objects we receive. In the next chapter, we will see how these interfaces are used in the following few chapters.

CHAPTER 17: MOVIEDATASERVICE: CONNECTING TO THE BACKEND

To retrieve the list of movies from the database, we will need to connect to our backend server. We will create a *service* class for that. A service is a class with a well-defined specific function your app needs. In our case, our service is responsible for talking to the backend to get and save data. Service classes provide their functionality to be consumed by components.

Components should be light-weight, mainly rendering views supported by application logic. They don't fetch data from the server or validate user input but rather delegate such tasks to services. We will cover more about components in the next chapter.

We will now create a service to connect to our backend server. Under *src/app*, create a new folder called *services*. In *services*, create a new file *movie.service.ts* with the following code:

```
import { HttpClient, HttpHeaders } from '@angular/common/http';
import { Injectable } from '@angular/core';
import { Observable } from 'rxjs';
import Movie from 'src/app/interfaces/movie';
import Movies from 'src/app/interfaces/movies';

@Injectable()
export class MovieDataService {
  constructor(private _http: HttpClient) {}

  find(query: string, by = 'title', page = 0): Observable<Movies> {
    return this._http.get<Movies>(
      `http://localhost:5000/api/v1/movies?${by}=${query}&page=${page}`
    );
  }

  get(id: string): Observable<Movie> {
    return this._http.get<Movie>(
      `http://localhost:5000/api/v1/movies/id/${id}`
    );
  }

  createReview(data: any) {
    return this._http.post<any>(
      'http://localhost:5000/api/v1/movies/review',
```

```
      data
    );
  }

  updateReview(data: any) {
    return    this._http.put('http://localhost:5000/api/v1/movies/review',
data);
  }

  deleteReview(review_id: string, user_id: string) {
    const options = {
      headers: new HttpHeaders({
        'Content-Type': 'application/json'
      }),
      body: {
        review_id: review_id,
        user_id: user_id
      }
    };
    return this._http.delete(
      'http://localhost:5000/api/v1/movies/review',
      options
    );
  }

  getRatings(): Observable<string[]> {
    return this._http.get<string[]>(
      'http://localhost:5000/api/v1/movies/ratings'
    );
  }
}
```

* Refer to the source code (www.greglim.co/p/mean) if you prefer to copy and paste

Code Explanation

```
import { HttpClient, HttpHeaders } from '@angular/common/http';
```

We import the *HttpClient* class in Angular to make requests to the server. The *HttpClient* class provides the *get()* method for getting a resource, *post()* for creating it, *put()* for updating it and *delete()* for deleting a resource. We will explain *HttpHeaders* in a later section.

```
import { Observable } from 'rxjs';
```

We import *Observables* which is an asynchronous data stream. We can subscribe to an *Observable* and get notified when data arrives asynchronously.

```
import { Injectable } from '@angular/core';
```

We import *Injectable* to mark our *MovieDataService* class (see below code) as available for dependency injection by the consuming component.

```
@Injectable()
export class MovieDataService {
  constructor(private _http: HttpClient) {}
```

Dependency injection supplies instances of classes you depend on. Angular will look at the types of a constructor's parameters, create an instance of the parameter type and inject it into the constructor. For e.g., in the above, we inject the *HttpClient* class into the constructor of *MovieDataService*. Angular creates an instance of *HttpClient* class and gives it to us. Our constructor has a parameter *_http* of type *HttpClient*. By convention, we prefix private fields with an underscore '_'.

The *MovieDataService* class contains functions which make the API calls to the backend endpoints (we have implemented earlier) and return the results.

```
find(query: string, by = 'title', page = 0): Observable<Movies> {
  return this._http.get<Movies>(
    `http://localhost:5000/api/v1/movies?${by}=${query}&page=${page}`
  );
}
```

find returns all the movies for a particular query string (user-entered search title or ratings), by which field to search (i.e. *title* or *rated*) and page (default page request is 0). We put the API URL into the *get* method. This endpoint is served by the method *apiGetMovies* in *MoviesController* (refer to chapter 8). The query string will be provided by the user from the frontend input which we will implement later. The return type of *get()* is an Observable of *<Movies>*. We have earlier defined the *Movies* interface in /src/app/models.ts. By specifying *<Movies>* type, we indicate the type of the response wrapped inside the Observable. We return this Observable to the component which subscribes to it. When the *get()* request is completed, the response is fed to th e Observable and pushed to the component.

```
get(id: string): Observable<Movie> {
  return this._http.get<Movie>(
    `http://localhost:5000/api/v1/movies/id/${id}`
  );
}
```

get(id: string) gets the specific movie with the supplied id. This endpoint is served by the method *apiGetMovieById* in *MoviesController* (refer to chapter 12).

The remaining four methods are for creating, updating and deleting a review and to get all ratings. We will revisit these methods and the entire flow from the frontend to the backend while implementing the Angular frontend.

app.module.ts

Before we move on, we have to import the *HttpClientModule* into *AppModule* as shown in **bold** below.

```
...
import { HttpClientModule } from '@angular/common/http';

@NgModule({
  declarations: [
    AppComponent,
    MoviesListComponent,
    MovieComponent,
    AddReviewComponent,
    LoginComponent
  ],
  imports: [
    BrowserModule,
    AppRoutingModule,
    HttpClientModule
  ],
  providers: [],
  bootstrap: [AppComponent]
})
export class AppModule { }
```

We need to import *HttpClientModule* because we are using *HttpClient*.

CHAPTER 18: MOVIESLIST COMPONENT

Let's now implement the *MoviesList* component to consume the functionality in *MovieDataService*. Remember that components are meant to mainly render views supported by application logic for better user experience. They don't fetch data from the backend but rather delegate such tasks to services.

We will carry on implementing our *MoviesList* component. Fill in the below code into *movies-list.component.ts*:

```
import { Component, OnDestroy, OnInit } from '@angular/core';
import { MovieDataService } from 'src/app/services/movie.service';
import Movie from 'src/app/interfaces/movie';
import { FormControl } from '@angular/forms';
import {filter,debounceTime,distinctUntilChanged} from 'rxjs/operators';
import { Subscription } from 'rxjs';

@Component({
  selector: 'app-movies-list',
  templateUrl: './movies-list.component.html',
  providers: [MovieDataService]
})
export class MoviesListComponent implements OnInit, OnDestroy {
  title = new FormControl('');
  ratingsDropdown = new FormControl();

  movies: Array<Movie> = [];
  ratings: Array<string> = [];

  subscriptionRatings!: Subscription;
  subscriptionMovies!: Subscription;
}
```

Code Explanation

As we explain the code, we will highlight the relevant imports.

```
  title = new FormControl('');
  ratingsDropdown = new FormControl();
```

We create two *FormControl* objects which represent the *title* field and *ratings* dropdown field. This will allow the user to enter their search criteria either by title or ratings.

```
movies: Array<Movie> = [];
ratings: Array<string> = [];

subscriptionRatings!: Subscription;
subscriptionMovies!: Subscription;
```

Next, we create a series of variables. The *movies* array will hold the movies to be displayed in the Movies List page. *ratings* array contains the list of values to populate the *ratings* dropdown.

ngOnInit to Retrieve Movies and Ratings

Next, we implement the *ngOnInit* lifecycle method. *ngOnInit* is called when our component is first instantiated. In terms of lifecycle, it is called after the constructor. In the constructor, we do lightweight and necessary initialization. For calls to the server, we do it in *ngOnInit*. Add the below *constructor* and *ngOnInit* into *movies-list.component.ts* (we add them as methods of the *MoviesListComponent* class):

```
constructor(private _movieDataService: MovieDataService) {}

ngOnInit() {
  this.subscriptionRatings = this._movieDataService.getRatings()
    .subscribe((data) => {
      this.ratings = data;
    });

  this.title.valueChanges.pipe(filter((text) => text.length >= 3),
    debounceTime(400),distinctUntilChanged())
      .subscribe((value) => {
        this.subscriptionMovies = this._movieDataService.find(value,"title")
        .subscribe((data) => {
          this.movies = data.movies;
        });
      }
    );
}
```

Code Explanation

```
  this.subscriptionRatings = this._movieDataService.getRatings()
    .subscribe((data) => {
      this.ratings = data;
    });
```

The above code calls *MovieDataService.getRatings()* which if you remember, has the following implementation:

```
getRatings(): Observable<string[]> {
  return this._http.get<string[]>(
    'http://localhost:5000/api/v1/movies/ratings'
  );
}
```

getRatings returns an Observable with the list of distinct ratings from the database. We subscribe to it and assign the returned ratings result to the *ratings* array.

```
this.title.valueChanges.pipe(filter((text) => text.length >= 3),
  debounceTime(400),distinctUntilChanged())
    .subscribe((value) => {
      this.subscriptionMovies = this._movieDataService.find(value,"title")
      .subscribe((data) => {
        this.movies = data.movies;
      });
    }
  );
```

In a similar fashion, the above code in **bold** calls *MovieDataService.find* to get the list of movies that fulfill the search criteria entered by the user.

In the next section, we will explain the purpose of the other code that surrounds *MovieDataService.find*.

Observable Operators

```
this.title.valueChanges.pipe(filter((text) => text.length >= 3),
  debounceTime(400),distinctUntilChanged())
    .subscribe((value) => {
      this.subscriptionMovies = this._movieDataService.find(value,"title")
      .subscribe((data) => {
        this.movies = data.movies;
      });
    }
  );
```

In the above code, what we are doing is each time user enters a search term into the *title* field, we call the *find* movies function. The *title formControl* class has the *valueChanges* property which returns an Observable. We subscribe to this Observable to get notified whenever the user types into the input field.

The benefit of Observables is that it provides a set of operators we can use to transform, filter, aggregate and combine data received from the observable stream.

filter Operator

We use the *filter* operator "`filter((text) => text.length >= 3)`" to ensure that we make a request only when the user types in at least three characters so as not to flood our backend with too many unnecessary requests. We import the *filter* operator with `import { filter } from 'rxjs/operators';`

The *filter* operator takes an expression *text.length >= 3* and determines that the value should be selected only if the expression returns true. We wrap the *filter* operator function call with the *pipe()* method. When we have more than one operator - in our case, *debounceTime* and *distinctUntilChanged*, the *pipe* method executes them from left to right.

debounceTime Operator

```
debounceTime(400)
```

We apply the *debounceTime* operator to wait 400 milliseconds in between requests before calling the backend. We importing the *debounceTime* operator with:

```
import { filter,debounceTime,distinctUntilChanged } from 'rxjs/operators';
```

The *pipe* method now contains the *filter* operator and the *debounceTime* operator. *pipe()* executes them from left to right meaning it executes *filter* first followed by *debounceTime*. Thus, you can see that the benefit of Observable operators is that you can keep applying operators for your own custom logic.

distinctUntilChanged Operator

```
distinctUntilChanged()
```

Say if a user presses the left and right arrow keys to move the cursor, the *valueChange* event is fired and we send multiple requests with the same input string since the text in the input field is not changed. To avoid such multiple requests with the same search term, we apply the *distinctUntilChanged* operator which let us receive our Observable only when the text is changed. We import the *distinctUntilChanged* operator with:

```
import { filter,debounceTime,distinctUntilChanged } from 'rxjs/operators';
```

Thus, using the *title's FormControl's valueChanges* Observable, we don't need to have a submit button for our search form. Each time the user types into the title field, it will detect the change and request from the backend.

But our *rating* dropdown *FormControl* currently does not detect a value change and requests from the backend. Let's do so by implementing the *changeRating* method (we add it as a method of the *MoviesListComponent* class):

```
changeRating(value: string){
  this.subscriptionMovies = this._movieDataService.find(value,"rated")
    .subscribe((data) => {
      this.movies = data.movies;
      console.log("ratingsDropdown",this.movies);
    });
}
```

ngOnDestroy

Additionally, to improve on memory, we implement *ngOnDestroy()* so that we remove the subscription object from memory when this component instance is destroyed. Implement the *ngOnDestroy* method with the following (we add it as a method of the *MoviesListComponent* class):

```
ngOnDestroy(): void {
  if (this.subscriptionRatings) {
    this.subscriptionRatings.unsubscribe();
  }
  if (this.subscriptionMovies) {
    this.subscriptionMovies.unsubscribe();
  }
}
```

app.module.ts

Before we move on, we have to import the *ReactiveFormsModule* into *AppModule* as shown in **bold** below.

```
...
import { ReactiveFormsModule} from '@angular/forms';

@NgModule({
  declarations: [
    AppComponent,
    MoviesListComponent,
    MovieComponent,
```

```
    AddReviewComponent,
    LoginComponent
  ],
  imports: [
    BrowserModule,
    AppRoutingModule,
    HttpClientModule,
    ReactiveFormsModule
  ],
  providers: [],
  bootstrap: [AppComponent]
})
export class AppModule { }
```

We need to import *ReactiveFormsModule* because we are using *FormControl*:

```
...
export class MoviesListComponent implements OnInit, OnDestroy {
  title = new FormControl('');
  ratingsDropdown = new FormControl();
...
```

MoviesList Component Template

Now, let's copy the markup of a simple form from the getbootstrap site (https://getbootstrap.com/docs/5.0/forms/form-control/) and put it into *movies-list.component.html*. It will look something like:

```
<h3>Movie Results</h3>
<div class="row">
    <div class="col">
        <div class="mb-3">
            <input
              id="title"
              class="form-control"
              [formControl]="title"
              placeholder="Search by title"
            >
        </div>
    </div>
    <div class="col">
```

```
<select
    class="form-select"
    #selectRating
    (change)="changeRating(selectRating.value)"
>
    <option selected>Select by Rating</option>
    <option *ngFor="let rating of ratings" [value]="rating">
        {{rating}}
    </option>
</select>
</div>
</div>
```

* Refer to the source code (www.greglim.co/p/mean) for the complete *MoviesListComponent* code.

Code Explanation

This creates a simple form with a search by title field and search by ratings dropdown. We have used `<div class="row">` and `<div class="col">` to put the two search fields in a single row and in side by side columns (fig. 1).

Movies Reviews   Movies   Login

Movie Results

| Search by title | | Select by Rating ⌄ |

Figure 1

```
<input
    id="title"
    class="form-control"
    [formControl]="title"
    placeholder="Search by title"
>
```

We use the *formControl* directive in the *input* control to bind it to the *title* FormControl in the *MoviesListComponent* class.

```
<select
    class="form-select"
    #selectRating
    (change)="changeRating(selectRating.value)"
```

```
>
    <option selected>Select by Rating</option>
    <option *ngFor="let rating of ratings" [value]="rating">
        {{rating}}
    </option>
</select>
```

We then have the 'Select by Rating' *FormControl* which is the dropdown field to select a movie rating. To populate the option values for the dropdown, we use *ngFor*, where for each *rating* in *ratings* array, we repeat an *option* element with the rating value for the select box (fig. 2).

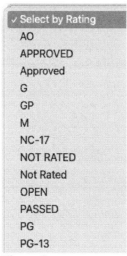

Figure 2

HTML Markup for Displaying Movies

Now, let's display the list of movies like in figure 3 (you need to include some code which is presented below).

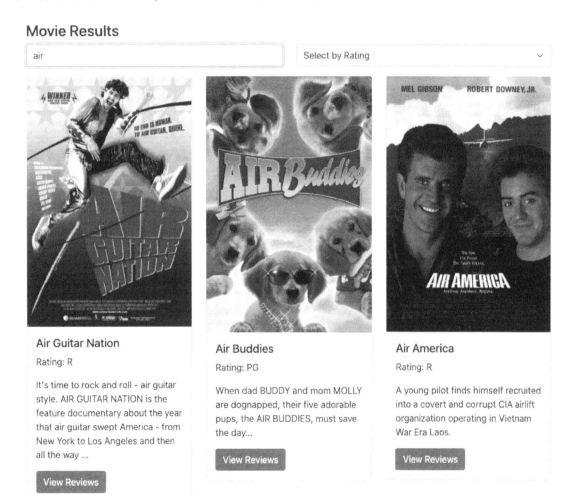

Figure 3

In *movies-list.component.html*, add the below code below the search form:

```
<h3>Movie Results</h3>
...
...
<div class="row row-cols-1 row-cols-md-3 g-4">
    <div class="col" *ngFor="let movie of movies">
      <div class="card">
        <img
            *ngIf="movie.poster"
            src="{{ movie.poster }}"
            class="card-img-top"
            alt="..."
        >
        <div class="card-body">
            <h5 class="card-title">{{ movie.title }}</h5>
            <p class="card-text">Rating: {{ movie.rated }}</p>
            <p class="card-text">{{ movie.plot }}</p>
            <a
                class="btn btn-primary"
                [routerLink]="['/movies/',movie._id]">
                View Reviews
            </a>
        </div>
      </div>
    </div>
</div>
```

Code Explanation

We use the *ngFor* function again where for each movie in *movies*, we return a *Card* component which we take from getbootstrap (https://getbootstrap.com/docs/5.0/components/card/ - fig. 4).

Air Buddies

Rating: PG

When dad BUDDY and mom MOLLY are
dognapped, their five adorable pups, the
AIR BUDDIES, must save the day...

View Reviews

Figure 4

Each Card contains one movie with its:
- poster image:

```
<img
    *ngIf="movie.poster"
    src="{{ movie.poster }}"
    class="card-img-top"
    alt="..."
>
```
- title: `<h5 class="card-title">{{ movie.title }}</h5>`
- rating: `<p class="card-text">Rating: {{ movie.rated }}</p>`
- plot: `<p class="card-text">{{ movie.plot }}</p>`
- "View Reviews" Link:

```
<a
    class="btn btn-primary"
    [routerLink]="['/movies/',movie._id]">
    View Reviews
</a>
```

109

You can view all of the movie's available properties back in MongoDB Atlas (fig. 5).

```
_id: ObjectId("573a1390f29313caabcd4135")
plot: "Three men hammer on an anvil and pass a bottle of beer around."
> genres: Array
  runtime: 1
> cast: Array
  num_mflix_comments: 1
  title: "Blacksmith Scene"
  fullplot: "A stationary camera looks at a large anvil with a blacksmith behind it..."
> countries: Array
  released: 1893-05-09T00:00:00.000+00:00
> directors: Array
  rated: "UNRATED"
> awards: Object
  lastupdated: "2015-08-26 00:03:50.133000000"
  year: 1893
> imdb: Object
  type: "movie"
> tomatoes: Object
```

Figure 5

Testing your App

When you run your app now, try entering search terms in 'Search by title' or 'Select by rating'. It will return the related results (fig. 6, 7, 8)!

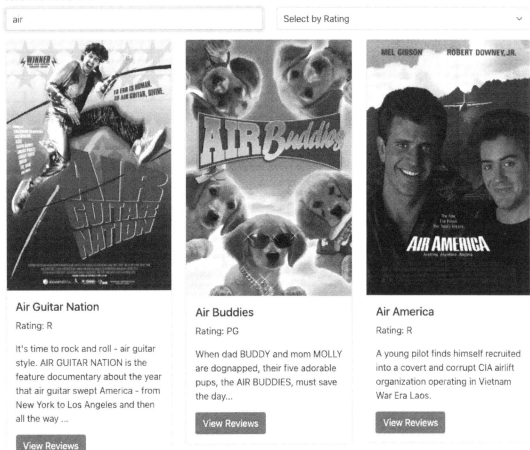

Figure 6

Note that some movies do not have a poster image which is why in the *img* tag, we add *ngIf* to display the image component only if there is a poster image.

```
<img
    *ngIf="movie.poster"
    src="{{ movie.poster }}"
    class="card-img-top"
    alt="..."
>
```

Movies Reviews   Movies   Login

Movie Results

| train| | | Select by Rating   ∨ |

The Train

Rating: UNRATED

In 1944, a German colonel loads a train with French art treasures to send to Germany. The Resistance must stop it without damaging the cargo.

View Reviews

Atomic Train

Rating: PG-13

A train filled with atomic devices threatens to destroy the city of Denver. John Serger (a train buff) has to prevent this from happening

View Reviews

Last Train to Freo

Rating:

Two thugs from the Perth suburb of Midland catch the last train to Fremantle. When a young woman boards the train a few stops later, they begin talking and find out not everyone on the train is who they seem to be.

View Reviews

Figure 7 - Results for search by title: 'train'

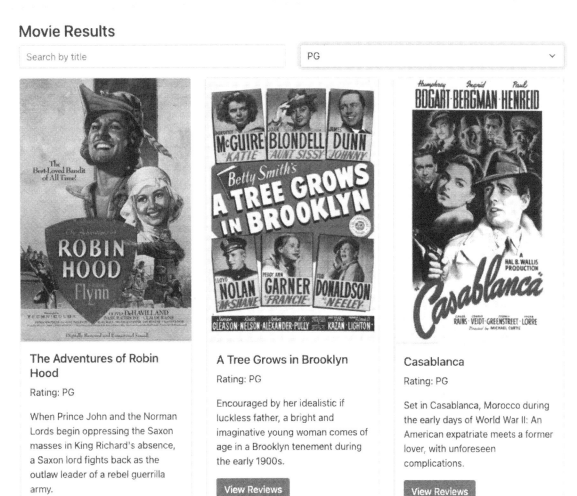

Figure 8 - Results for search by rating: 'PG'

Currently, we are displaying just the first twenty results. Later on, we will consider how to retrieve the next page's results. Now, let's carry on with viewing the reviews of a particular movie in a Movie Component.

* Refer to the source code (www.greglim.co/p/mean) for the complete code of *movies-list.component.ts*

CHAPTER 19: MOVIE COMPONENT

Currently, when we click on 'View Reviews', it just shows a message. We will create a *Movie* component which shows the individual movie along with its reviews.

In the *components/movie* folder, in *movie.component.ts*, fill in the following code:

```
import { Component, OnInit, OnDestroy } from '@angular/core';
import { MovieDataService } from '../../services/movie.service';
import { ActivatedRoute, Router } from '@angular/router';
import { Subscription } from 'rxjs';
import Movie from 'src/app/interfaces/movie';

@Component({
  selector: 'app-movie',
  templateUrl: './movie.component.html',
  providers: [MovieDataService]
})
export class MovieComponent implements OnInit, OnDestroy {
  id = '';
  subscription!: Subscription;
  movie: Movie = {
    poster: '',
    title: '',
    rated: '',
    plot: '',
    _id: '',
    reviews: []
  };

  constructor(
    private _movieDataService: MovieDataService,
    private _route: ActivatedRoute,
    private _router: Router
  ) {}

  ngOnInit(): void {
    this.subscription = this._route.params.subscribe((params) => {
      this.id = params['id'];
      this._movieDataService.get(this.id).subscribe((data) => {
        this.movie = data;
```

```
      });
    });
  }

  ngOnDestroy(): void {
    if (this.subscription) {
      this.subscription.unsubscribe();
    }
  }
}
```

Code Explanation

```
  id = '';
  subscription!: Subscription;
  movie: Movie = {
    poster: '',
    title: '',
    rated: '',
    plot: '',
    _id: '',
    reviews: []
  };
```

We have a *movie* variable to hold the specific movie we are currently showing in the Movie component. We set its initial values to empty strings ("") or an empty array *[]*.

```
  constructor(
    private _movieDataService: MovieDataService,
    private _route: ActivatedRoute,
    private _router: Router
  ) {}
```

We use dependency injection to get an instance of *MovieDataService*, *ActivatedRoute*, and *Router*. *ActivatedRoute* contains route information of a component and we subscribe to its *params* method to get our route parameters as shown below:

```
ngOnInit(): void {
  this.subscription = this._route.params.subscribe((params) => {
    this.id = params['id'];
    this._movieDataService.get(this.id).subscribe((data) => {
      this.movie = data;
    });
  });
}
```

In the *ngOnInit* method (remember that *ngOnInit* is called when the component renders), we subscribe to *_route.params* which returns an Observable. We get the value of the parameters using `this.id = params['id']`. We then call *get()* of *MovieDataService* (refer to chapter 17) which in turn calls the API route:

```
get(id){
    return axios.get(`http://localhost:5000/api/v1/movies/id/${id}`);
}
```

Now, where did we populate `params id`?

Remember back in *MoviesListComponent*, we have the "View Reviews" link to route to the *Movie* component:

```
<a
        class="btn btn-primary"
        [routerLink]="['/movies/',movie._id]">
        View Reviews
</a>
```

The route includes an *id* parameter for the movie id. So the route to get a specific movie will be something like: http://localhost:5000/movies/id/573a1390f29313caabcd6223

`params["id"]` will then give us *573a1390f29313caabcd6223*.

Movie Component Markup

Next, let's implement the frontend for the movie component. The frontend will look something like (fig. 1):

117

Figure 1

In *components/movie/movie.component.html*, fill in the below markup:

```html
<div class="row">
  <div class="col">
    <img
        *ngIf="movie.poster"
        src="{{ movie.poster }}"
        class="card-img-top" alt="..."
    >
  </div>
  <div class="col">
    <div class="card-body">
        <h5 class="card-title">{{ movie.title }}</h5>
        <p class="card-text">{{ movie.plot }}</p>
            <a
              class="btn btn-primary"
              [routerLink]="['/movies/review',movie._id]">
              Add Reviews
            </a>
    </div>
  </div>
</div>
```

Code Explanation

We essentially have two columns.

```
<div class="col">
  <img
      *ngIf="movie.poster"
      src="{{ movie.poster }}"
      class="card-img-top" alt="..."
  >
</div>
<div class="col">
  <div class="card-body">
     ...
  </div>
</div>
```

The first column contains the movie poster (if it exists) and the second column show the movie details in a Card component.

```
<a
  class="btn btn-primary"
  [routerLink]="['/movies/review',movie._id]">
  Add Reviews
</a>
```

In the Card component, we render a 'Add Review' button which routes to the *AddReviewComponent*. Adding a review should only be allowed to logged-in users. In a later chapter, we will implement it such that only if the user is logged in, we render the "Add Reviews" button. For now, we will proceed with implementing the listing of reviews.

CHAPTER 20: LISTING REVIEWS

We will be listing the reviews under the movie plot (fig. 1).

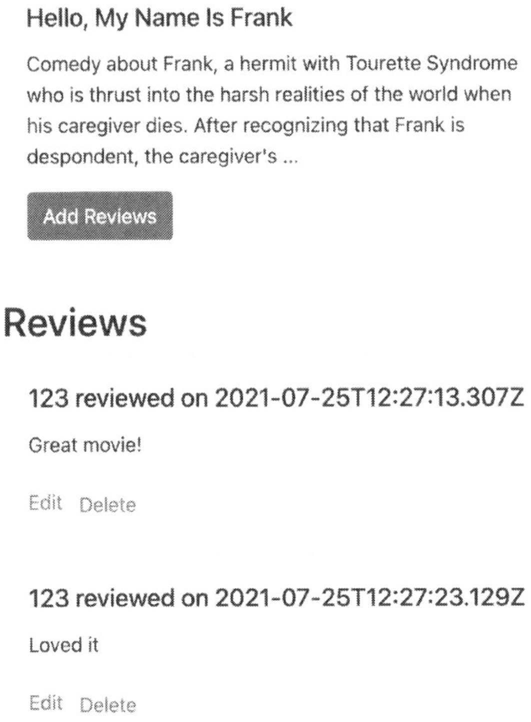

Hello, My Name Is Frank

Comedy about Frank, a hermit with Tourette Syndrome who is thrust into the harsh realities of the world when his caregiver dies. After recognizing that Frank is despondent, the caregiver's ...

Add Reviews

Reviews

123 reviewed on 2021-07-25T12:27:13.307Z

Great movie!

Edit   Delete

123 reviewed on 2021-07-25T12:27:23.129Z

Loved it

Edit   Delete

Figure 1

To do so, in *components/movie/movie.component.html*, add the below mark up in **bold**:

```
<div class="row">
  <div class="col">
  ...
  </div>
  <div class="col">
    <div class="card-body">
    ...
    </div>
    <h2>Reviews</h2>
    <div *ngFor="let review of movie.reviews">
```

```
<div class="card border-light">
  <div class="card-body">
    <h5 class="card-title">
      {{ review.name }} reviewed on {{ review.date }}
    </h5>
    <p class="card-text">{{ review.review }}</p>
      <a class="card-link">
            Edit
      </a>
      <button
            type="button"
            class="btn btn-link"
      >
            Delete
      </button>
    </div>
  </div>
</div>
</div>
```

Code Explanation

We access the *reviews* array and using *ngFor*, for each review, render a *Card* component with title, review text, *Edit* and *Delete* buttons (fig. 2).

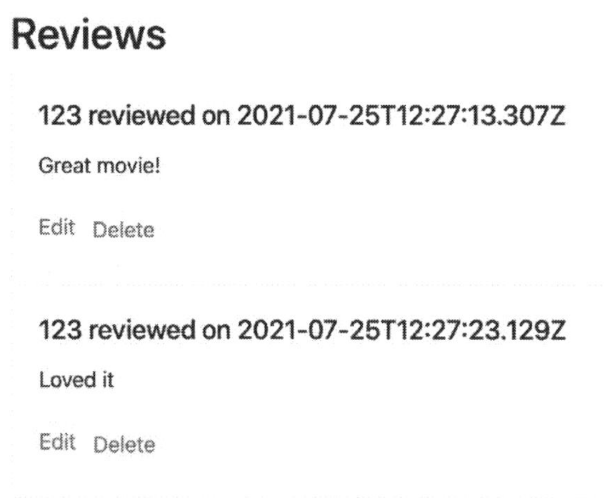

Reviews

123 reviewed on 2021-07-25T12:27:13.307Z

Great movie!

Edit Delete

123 reviewed on 2021-07-25T12:27:23.129Z

Loved it

Edit Delete

Figure 2

Later on, we will implement such that a logged-in user can only edit/delete reviews they have posted. They can't delete/edit other's reviews.

Testing our App

If you test your app, now, you will be able to go to a specific movie page and see its reviews with its Edit/Delete buttons.

Formatting the Date

Before we go on to the next chapter, our current review date is in timestamp format e.g. *2021-05-10T00:08:50.082Z*. Let's format the review date(s) into a presentable manner. We will be using a library called *moment js*, a lightweight JavaScript library for parsing, validating and formatting dates.

In Terminal, in your project directory, install *moment js* with:

```
npm i moment --save
```

In *movie.component.ts*, import moment with:

```
...
import * as moment from 'moment';
...
```

Therefore, create the *getFormattedDate(date: Date)* method inside the *MovieComponent* class. This method receives a Date and transforms it into a presentable manner.

```
getFormattedDate(date: Date) {
  return moment(date).format("Do MMMM YYYY");
}
```

Then, use the *getFormattedDate* method inside the *movie.component.html* file to pass and transform the review date value:

```
<h5 class="card-title">
{{ review.name }} reviewed on {{ getFormattedDate(review.date) }}
</h5>
```

And when you run your app, the review dates should be nicely formatted (fig. 3).

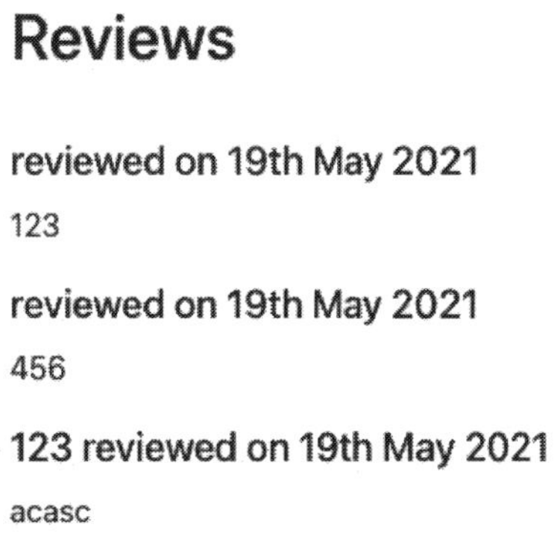

Reviews

reviewed on 19th May 2021

123

reviewed on 19th May 2021

456

123 reviewed on 19th May 2021

acasc

Figure 3

Chapter 21: Login Service

We won't be doing a full feature authentication system as it is outside the scope of this book, but it will be a preliminary template for you to fill in your own full-fledged login using Google sign-in, Firebase, OAuth or other authentication providers.

Under *src/app/service/*, create a new file *login.service.ts*. This will be the service class for login functionality. Remember that we should implement logic in service classes to keep our component classes lightweight and mainly for rendering displays. Fill in *login.service.ts* with the below code:

```
import { Injectable } from '@angular/core';
import User from 'src/app/interfaces/user';
import { Subject } from 'rxjs';

/* mark our Login service class as available for dependency injection with
@Injectable() annotation. */

@Injectable()
export class LoginService {
  user: User = {
    name: '',
    id: ''
  };

  userChange: Subject<User> = new Subject<User>();

  constructor() {
    this.userChange.subscribe((value) => {
      this.user = value;
    });
  }

  login(name = '', id = '') {
    this.userChange.next({ name: name, id: id });
  }

  logout() {
    this.userChange.next({ name: '', id: '' });
  }
}
```

Code Explanation

```
user: User = {
  name: '',
  id: ''
};
```

Our login service class is a simple class with a user object with *name* and *id* properties. They contain the name and id of the current logged-in user. If there is no user logged-in, *name* and *id* will be set to empty strings.

```
userChange: Subject<User> = new Subject<User>();
```

We have a RxJS *Subject* which is a special type of Observable that allows values to be multicasted to Observers. We need *Subject* of *User* type so that when a user logs in, we can then emit the logged-in user information to other components who need it. For e.g., *AppComponent* so that it can change the navbar from 'login' to 'logout user'.

```
login(name = '', id = '') {
  this.userChange.next({ name: name, id: id });
}
```

We have a method *login* that takes in *username* and *id* credentials. In a real application, our *login* method should call an authentication API on a server with the credentials before calling *userChange.next*.

We feed the logged-in user object to *userChange.next* to multicast it to the Observers who have subscribed.

```
constructor() {
  this.userChange.subscribe((value) => {
    this.user = value;
  });
}
```

In the constructor, we start subscribing to *userChange* so that the *user* object can be updated upon login or logout.

```
logout() {
  this.userChange.next({ name: '', id: '' });
}
```

The *logout* method simply sets the name and id to empty strings to represent that no user is logged-in currently.

Lastly, note that whenever we create a new service class and want to use it, we should specify it in the *providers* array of our module class to state that we want to use it in that module. In our case, since we have only one module *AppModule*, we import and specify it in *providers: [LoginService]* of *app.module.ts*:

```
...
import { LoginService } from './services/login.service';

@NgModule({
  declarations: [
      ...
  ],
  imports: [
      ...
  ],
  providers: [LoginService],
  bootstrap: [AppComponent]
})
export class AppModule { }
```

With *LoginService*, it facilitates us to pass the logged-in *user* to other components e.g. *AddReview*, *Movie* as we shall see later.

In the next chapter, we will implement the Login Component.

CHAPTER 22: LOGGING IN

In *src/app/components/login/*, fill in *login.component.ts* with the following code:

```
import { Component, OnInit } from '@angular/core';
import { FormGroup, FormControl } from '@angular/forms';
import { LoginService } from '../../services/login.service';
import { Router } from '@angular/router';

@Component({
  selector: 'app-login',
  templateUrl: './login.component.html',
  styleUrls: ['./login.component.css']
})
export class LoginComponent implements OnInit {
  form = new FormGroup({
    name: new FormControl(''),
    id: new FormControl('')
  });

  constructor(private _loginService: LoginService, private _router:
Router) {}

  login() {
    this._loginService.login(
      this.form.controls['name'].value,
      this.form.controls['id'].value
    );

    if (
      this._loginService.user.name.length > 0 &&
      this._loginService.user.id.length > 0
    ) {
      // route to homepage
      this._router.navigate(['/']);
    }
  }

  ngOnInit(): void {}
}
```

* Refer to the source code (www.greglim.co/p/mean) if you prefer to copy and paste

Code Explanation

```
form = new FormGroup({
  name: new FormControl(''),
  id: new FormControl('')
});
```

Using *FormGroup*, we have a simple login form with *name* and *id* FormControls. We set the initial value of *name* and *id* to be empty strings (").

```
login() {
  this._loginService.login(
    this.form.controls['name'].value,
    this.form.controls['id'].value
  );

  if (
    this._loginService.user.name.length > 0 &&
    this._loginService.user.id.length > 0
  ) {
    // route to homepage
    this._router.navigate(['/']);
  }
}
```

When the user clicks on the Submit button (to be implemented in the template), it calls *login()*. We retrieve the user entered values from the *name* and *id* form control and pass it to the LoginService's *login* method implemented in the last chapter.

We then check for successful login if *LoginService* user's name and id fields are populated. If so, we redirect to the main page with `this._router.navigate(['/'])`. Next, let's implement *login.component.html*.

login.component.html

Fill in *login.component.html* with the following:

```
<form [formGroup]="form" (ngSubmit)="login()">
    <div class="mb-3">
    <label for="name" class="form-label">Name</label>
    <input
        type="text"
        class="form-control"
        id="name"
        placeholder="Enter username"
        formControlName="name"
    >
    </div>
    <div class="mb-3">
        <label for="id">ID</label>
        <input
            type="text"
            class="form-control"
            id="id"
            placeholder="Enter id"
            formControlName="id"
        >
    </div>
    <div class="mb-3">
    <button type="submit" class="btn btn-primary mb-3">Submit</button>
    </div>
</form>
```

As you can see, it is just a simple form with *name*, *id* form controls and *Submit* button.

Rendering Login/Logout in AppComponent's Navbar

Next, back in the Navbar of App Component, if the user is not logged in, we will show 'Login' which links to the login component.

Movies Reviews   Movies   Login

If the user is logged in, it will show 'Logout User' which calls the *logout* function.

Movies Reviews   Movies   Logout 123

app.component.ts

But first, we need to import *LoginService* in *AppComponent*. Remove the existing content in *app.component.ts* and fill it in with the below code:

```
import { Component } from '@angular/core';
import { LoginService } from './services/login.service';
import User from 'src/app/interfaces/user';

@Component({
  selector: 'app-root',
  templateUrl: './app.component.html',
  styleUrls: ['./app.component.css']
})
export class AppComponent {
  constructor(private _loginService: LoginService) {}

  ngOnInit(): void {}

  get userInfo(): User {
    return this._loginService.user;
  }

  logout() {
    this._loginService.logout();
  }
}
```

Code Explanation

get userInfo is simply a getter method to expose the *LoginService*'s *user* object for use in our template. *logout()* simply call's LoginService's *logout* function.

app.component.html

In the navbar, to display 'Login' if user is not logged in and display 'Logout User' otherwise, add the following in *app.component.html*.

```
<nav class="navbar navbar-expand-lg navbar-light bg-light">
  <div class="container-fluid">
    <a class="navbar-brand" routerLink="movies">Movies Reviews</a>
    <button class="navbar-toggler" type="button">
      <span class="navbar-toggler-icon"></span>
    </button>
    <div class="collapse navbar-collapse">
      <ul class="navbar-nav me-auto mb-2 mb-lg-0">
        <li class="nav-item">
          <a class="nav-link active" routerLink="movies">Movies</a>
        </li>
        <li class="nav-item">
          <div *ngIf="userInfo.name.length > 0 && userInfo.id.length > 0;
            else elseBlock">
          <a class="nav-link" (click)="logout()">
            Logout {{ userInfo.name }}
          </a>
        </div>
        <ng-template #elseBlock>
          <a class="nav-link" routerLink="login">Login</a>
        </ng-template>
      </li>
    </ul>
  </div>
</div>
</nav>
<div class="container mt-3">
  <router-outlet></router-outlet>
</div>
```

Using *ngIf*, we check if *userInfo* has a populated name and id. If so, render "Logout" with the logged-in user's name. Else, simply display "Login".

"Logout" when clicked calls *logout()*. "Login" when clicked routes to the *LoginComponent*.

Rendering AddReview in MovieComponent

Having implemented *LoginService* and *LoginComponent*, we will enforce that only a logged-in user can add reviews. Additionally, logged-in users can only delete/edit reviews they have posted. They can't delete/edit other's reviews.

To implement that only a logged-in user can add reviews, in *movie.component.html*, add the codes in **bold**:

```
<div class="row">
  ...

  ...
  <div class="col">
    <div class="card-body">
        <h5 class="card-title">{{ movie.title }}</h5>
        <p class="card-text">{{ movie.plot }}</p>
        <div *ngIf="userInfo.name.length > 0 &&
            userInfo.id.length > 0">
          <a
            class="btn btn-primary"
            [routerLink]="['/movies/review',movie._id]">
            Add Reviews
          </a>
        </div>
      </div>
    </div>
  </div>
  ...
  ...
  ...
```

And add the below getter for *userInfo* to *movie.component.ts* by adding the codes in **bold**:

```
...
import User from 'src/app/interfaces/user';
import { LoginService } from 'src/app/services/login.service';
...
...

  constructor(
      private _movieDataService: MovieDataService,
      private _route: ActivatedRoute,
      private _router: Router,
      private _loginService: LoginService
  ) {}

  get userInfo(): User {
    return this._loginService.user;
  }
```

134

We display the "Add Reviews" button only if user name and id is populated.

Rendering Delete/Edit Reviews in MovieComponent

To implement that logged-in users can only delete/edit reviews they have posted and can't delete/edit other's reviews, in *movie.component.html*, add the codes in **bold**:

```
      ...
        ...
      <h2>Reviews</h2>
      <div *ngFor="let review of movie.reviews">
        <div class="card border-light">
          <div class="card-body">
            <h5 class="card-title">
              {{ review.name }} reviewed on {{ review.date }}
            </h5>
            <p class="card-text">{{ review.review }}</p>
            <div *ngIf="userInfo.id.length > 0 &&
              userInfo.id === review.user_id">
              <a class="card-link">
                    Edit
              </a>
              <button
                    type="button"
                    class="btn btn-link"
              >
                    Delete
              </button>
            </div>
          </div>
        </div>
      </div>
        ...
        ...
```

Only if the logged-in user id is the same as the review user id (`userInfo.id === review.user_id`), do we render the Edit/Delete buttons.

Testing your App

In your app, try logging in. The navbar of App Component should show 'Logout User' and 'Login' when the user logs out. In addition, go to a specific movie with reviews (refer back to chapter 11 on how to create reviews via Insomnia) and you will be able to see the Edit/Delete buttons for each review (fig. 1).

Figure 1

CHAPTER 23: ADDING AND EDITING REVIEWS

Now, let's go on to implement adding a review. When a user logs in, goes to a specific movie page and clicks 'Add Review' (fig. 1), we will render the *AddReview* component for the user to submit a review (fig. 2).

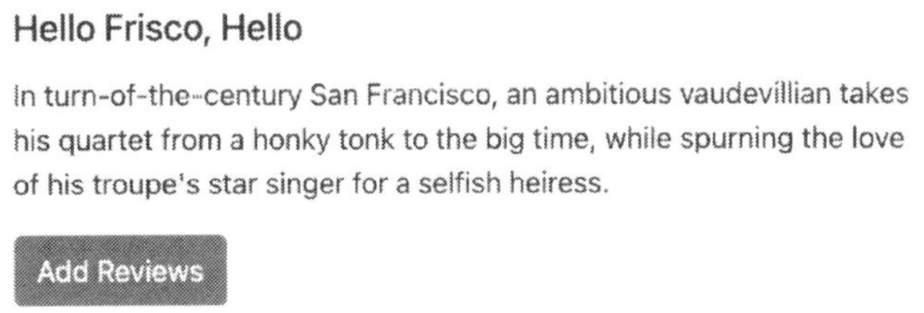

Hello Frisco, Hello

In turn-of-the-century San Francisco, an ambitious vaudevillian takes his quartet from a honky tonk to the big time, while spurning the love of his troupe's star singer for a selfish heiress.

Add Reviews

Figure 1

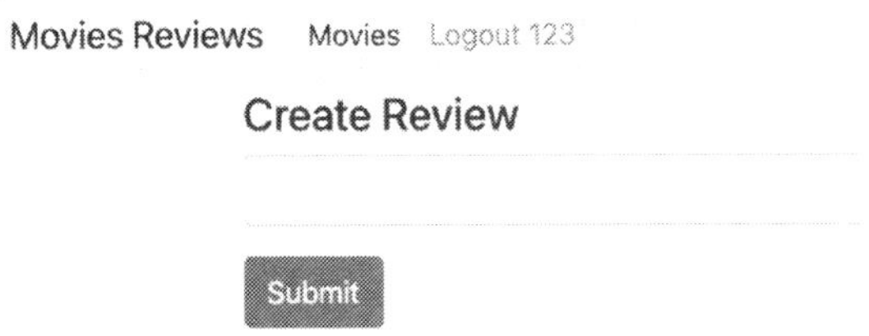

Movies Reviews   Movies   Logout 123

Create Review

Submit

Figure 2

We will also use the *AddReview* component to edit a review. That is, when a user clicks on the 'Edit' link on an existing review (fig. 3).

123 reviewed on 2021-07-27T10:42:31.091Z

nice

Edit Delete

Figure 3

When editing, we will render the *AddReview* component but with the header 'Edit Review' (fig. 4). The existing review text will be shown where users can then edit and submit.

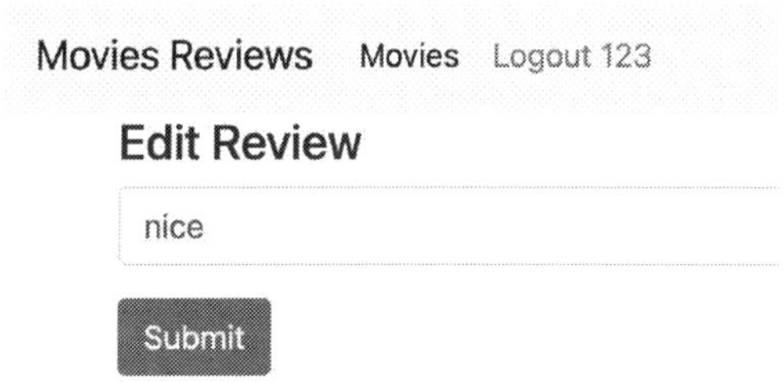

Movies Reviews   Movies   Logout 123

Edit Review

nice

Submit

Figure 4

So, our *AddReview* component will allow us to both add and edit reviews. Let's first go through the code to add a review.

Adding a Review

In *add-review.component.ts*, fill in the following code:

```
import { Component, OnInit, Input, OnDestroy } from '@angular/core';
import { ActivatedRoute } from '@angular/router';
import { Subscription } from 'rxjs';
import { LoginService } from '../../services/login.service';
import { MovieDataService } from '../../services/movie.service';
import { FormGroup, FormControl } from '@angular/forms';

@Component({
  selector: 'app-add-review',
  templateUrl: './add-review.component.html',
  providers: [MovieDataService]
})
export class AddReviewComponent implements OnInit, OnDestroy {
  editing = false;
  id = '';
  subscriptionParams!: Subscription;
  subscriptionMovieService!: Subscription;
  submitted = false;

  form = new FormGroup({
    review: new FormControl('')
  });

  constructor(
    private _route: ActivatedRoute,
```

```
    private _loginService: LoginService,
    private _movieDataService: MovieDataService
  ) {
    this.subscriptionParams = this._route.params.subscribe((params) => {
      this.id = params['id'];
    });
  }

  ngOnInit(): void {}

  saveReview() {
    const data = {
      review: this.form.controls['review'].value,
      name: this._loginService.user.name,
      user_id: this._loginService.user.id,
      movie_id: this.id, // get movie id direct from url
      review_id: ''
    };

    this.subscriptionMovieService = this._movieDataService
      .createReview(data)
      .subscribe((response) => {
        this.submitted = true;
      });
  }

  ngOnDestroy() {
    if (this.subscriptionParams) {
      this.subscriptionParams.unsubscribe();
    }

    if (this.subscriptionMovieService) {
      this.subscriptionMovieService.unsubscribe();
    }
  }
}
```
* Refer to the source code (www.greglim.co/p/mean) if you prefer to copy and paste

Code Explanation

```
editing = false;
id = '';
subscriptionParams!: Subscription;
subscriptionMovieService!: Subscription;
submitted = false;
```

The *editing* Boolean variable will be set to 'true' if the component is in 'Editing' mode. 'False' means we are adding a review.

We have a *submitted* state variable to keep track if the review is submitted.

```
form = new FormGroup({
  review: new FormControl('')
});
```

We have a *review* FormControl for the user to add/edit the review.

```
saveReview() {
  const data = {
    review: this.form.controls['review'].value,
    name: this._loginService.user.name,
    user_id: this._loginService.user.id,
    movie_id: this.id, // get movie id direct from url
    review_id: ''
  };

  this.subscriptionMovieService = this._movieDataService
    .createReview(data)
    .subscribe((response) => {
      this.submitted = true;
    });
}
```

saveReview is called by the submit button in the template. In *saveReview*, we first create a *data* object containing the review's properties, e.g. the review text, name and id of user who posted the review.

```
    name: this._loginService.user.name,
    user_id: this._loginService.user.id,
```

We get *name* and *user_id* from the *LoginService*'s *user* object.

```
constructor(
  private _route: ActivatedRoute,
  private _loginService: LoginService,
  private _movieDataService: MovieDataService
) {
  this.subscriptionParams = this._route.params.subscribe((params) => {
    this.id = params['id'];
  });
}
```

We get movie_id (`movie_id: this.id`) direct from the URL back in *movie.component.html*:

```
<a class="btn btn-primary" [routerLink]="['/movies/review',movie._id]">
     Add Reviews
</a>
```

We then call `MovieDataService.createReview(data)` which we implemented earlier in *movie.service.ts* with the following code:

```
createReview(data: any) {
  return this._http.post<any>(
    'http://localhost:5000/api/v1/movies/review',
    data
  );
}
```

This routes to *ReviewsController* in our backend and calls **apiPostReview** which then extracts *data* from the request's *body* parameter.

```
import ReviewsDAO from '../dao/ReviewsDAO.js';

export default class ReviewsController {
  static async apiPostReview(req, res, next) {
    try {
      const movieId = req.body.movie_id;
      const { review } = req.body;
      const userInfo = {
        name: req.body.name,
        _id: req.body.user_id,
      };
...
```

141

Hopefully, you can see better how the whole flow in a MEAN stack works now. Let's implement *app-review.component.html* next.

add-review.component.html

Fill in the below codes into *add-review.component.html*:

```
<div *ngIf="submitted ; else elseBlock">
    <h4>Review submitted successfully</h4>
    <a class="btn btn-primary" [routerLink]="['/movies/',id]">
        Back to Movie
    </a>
</div>
<ng-template #elseBlock>
    <form [formGroup]="form" (ngSubmit)="saveReview()">
        <div class="mb-3">
            <div *ngIf="editing ; else elseBlockReview">
                <h4>Edit Review </h4>
            </div>
            <ng-template #elseBlockReview>
                <h4>Create Review </h4>
            </ng-template>
            <input
              type="text"
              class="form-control"
              id="review"
              formControlName="review">
        </div>
        <div class="mb-3">
            <button
              type="submit"
              class="btn btn-primary mb-3">
              Submit
            </button>
        </div>
    </form>
</ng-template>
```

142

Code Explanation

```
<div *ngIf="submitted ; else elseBlock">
    <h4>Review submitted successfully</h4>
    <a class="btn btn-primary" [routerLink]="['/movies/',id]">
        Back to Movie
    </a>
</div>
```

We first have the section that when user has submitted the form, (we check with `ngIf="submitted`), render a 'Back to Movie' link for the user to route back to the Movie page.

If the user has not submitted the form, we render the 'elseBlock' to display the *saveReview* form.

```
<ng-template #elseBlock>
    <form [formGroup]="form" (ngSubmit)="saveReview()">
        ...
    </form>
</ng-template>
```

In the form, we check if its in 'editing' mode:

```
<div *ngIf="editing ; else elseBlockReview">
    <h4>Edit Review </h4>
</div>
<ng-template #elseBlockReview>
    <h4>Create Review </h4>
</ng-template>
```

If so, render the Form header to be 'Edit Review'. Else, render 'Create Review'.

```
<input
  type="text"
  class="form-control"
  id="review"
  formControlName="review">
</div>
<div class="mb-3">
    <button
      type="submit"
```

```
            class="btn btn-primary mb-3">
            Submit
        </button>
    </div>
```

Lastly, we render the *review* field form control. Let's go on to implement editing a review.

Editing a Review

We are currently just rendering an 'Edit' button in the Movie component *movie.component.ts*. Let's now implement its functionality by adding the below in **bold**:

```
        ...
        ...
        <a
            class="card-link"
            [routerLink]="['/movies/review',movie._id]"
            [state]="{ data: { review:review }}">
            Edit
        </a>
    ...
    ...
```

When a user clicks on the 'Edit' link, she is routed to the *AddReview* Component with the movie id as parameter. We also pass in a *state* object. *state* contains a *data* object which in turn contains the existing *review* object.

Back in *add-review.component.ts*, to retrieve the *state* and *review* object passed in, add in the below code to *ngOnInit*:

```
ngOnInit(): void {
  if (history.state.data) {
    this.editing = true;
    this.form.setValue({ review: history.state.data.review.review });
  }
}
```

And to *saveReview*:

```
saveReview() {
  const data = {
    review: this.form.controls['review'].value,
    name: this._loginService.user.name,
    user_id: this._loginService.user.id,
    movie_id: this.id, // get movie id direct from url
    review_id: ''
  };

  if (this.editing) {
    data.review_id = history.state.data.review._id;
    this.subscriptionMovieService = this._movieDataService
      .updateReview(data)
      .subscribe((response) => {
        this.submitted = true;
      });
  } else {
    this.subscriptionMovieService = this._movieDataService
      .createReview(data)
      .subscribe((response) => {
        this.submitted = true;
      });
  }
}
```

Code Explanation

```
ngOnInit(): void {
  if (history.state.data) {
    this.editing = true;
    this.form.setValue({ review: history.state.data.review.review });
  }
}
```

The *state* object is present under the *state* property of the *window*'s *history* object. We check if a state is passed into *AddReview*. Recall in *movie.component.html*, we pass in a state in the link to *Edit*:

```
            <a
                class="card-link"
                [routerLink]="['/movies/review',movie._id]"
                [state]="{ data: { review:review }}">
                Edit
            </a>
```

Thus, in *AddReview*, we check if a state is passed in and contains a *data* object. If so, set *editing* to true and set the form's *review* form control to the review object's review text.

```
if (this.editing) {
  data.review_id = history.state.data.review._id;
  this.subscriptionMovieService = this._movieDataService
    .updateReview(data)
    .subscribe((response) => {
      this.submitted = true;
    });
}
```

And if *editing* is true, we get the existing review id and call *updateReview* in *MovieDataService*:

```
updateReview(data: any) {
  return this._http.put(
        'http://localhost:5000/api/v1/movies/review', data
  );
}
```

The above calls the *apiUpdateReview* method in *ReviewsController* in the backend similar to how we call *apiPostReview* for adding a review:

```
static async apiUpdateReview(req, res, next) {
  try {
    const reviewId = req.body.review_id;
    const { review } = req.body;

    const date = new Date();

    const ReviewResponse = await ReviewsDAO.updateReview(
      reviewId,
      req.body.user_id,
      review,
      date,
    );
    ...
```

If you recall, **apiUpdateReview** extracts the *movieId* and *review* text similar to what we have done in posting a review and then calls *updateReview* and pass in the user_id to ensure that the user who is updating the view is the one who has created it.

Running our App

Now, let's run our app. Log in and go to a movie of your choice. Click on the 'Add Review' link and you should be able to add a review. The new review should appear in the movie page (fig. 5).

Figure 5

Having added the review, and if you are logged in, you will be able to edit the review by clicking on the 'Edit' link (fig. 6). And if you check your MongoDB, the data is updated there.

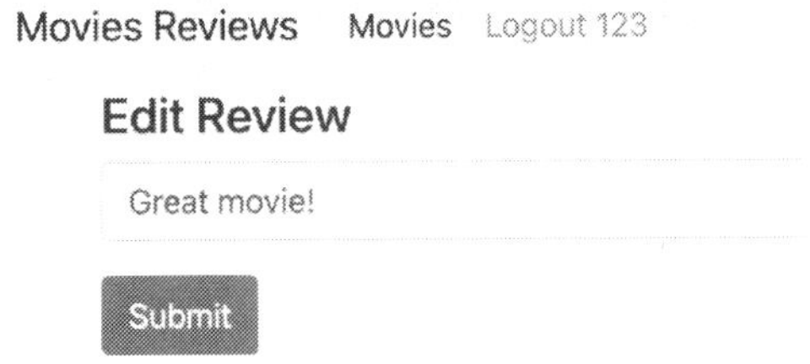

Figure 6

And you go back to your app and logout, you can't see the edit and delete buttons anymore. Next, we will finish up the implementation of deleting a review.

CHAPTER 24: DELETING A REVIEW

We are currently just rendering a delete button in the Movie component *movie.component.html*. Let's now implement its functionality by adding the below in **bold**:

```
<button
    type="button"
    class="btn btn-link"
    (click)="deleteReview(review._id)"
>
    Delete
</button>
```

We pass in the review id into *deleteReview*. Next, add in the below codes to implement *deleteReview* method in the *movie.component.ts* file:

```
deleteReview(reviewId: string) {
  this._movieDataService
    .deleteReview(reviewId, this._loginService.user.id)
    .subscribe((response) => {
      this.movie.reviews = this.movie.reviews.filter(
        ({ _id }) => _id !== reviewId
      );
    });
}
```

deleteReview then calls *deleteReview* in *MovieDataService*:

```
deleteReview(review_id: string, user_id: string) {
  const options = {
    headers: new HttpHeaders({
      'Content-Type': 'application/json'
    }),
    body: {
      review_id: review_id,
      user_id: user_id
    }
  };
  return this._http.delete(
    'http://localhost:5000/api/v1/movies/review',
    options
  );
}
```

We construct a HTTP header and *body* (containing id of review to be deleted and user id) for the delete HTTP request call to the *delete* API endpoint.

Remember that the *delete* endpoint is supported by *apiDeleteReview* in *ReviewsController* in the backend:

```
static async apiDeleteReview(req, res, next) {
  try {
    const reviewId = req.body.review_id;
    const userId = req.body.user_id;
    console.log('apiDeleteReview', req.body);
    const ReviewResponse = await ReviewsDAO.deleteReview(
      reviewId,
      userId,
    );
  ...
```

Back in *movie.component.ts*, we have a callback function that is called when *deleteReview* completes:

```
deleteReview(reviewId: string){
  this._movieDataService.deleteReview(
    reviewId,
    this._loginService.user.id)
    .subscribe(response => {
      this.movie.reviews = this.movie.reviews.filter(
        ({ _id }) => _id !== reviewId
      );
    })
}
```

In the callback, *filter()* creates a new array with all elements that pass the test implemented by the provided function i.e. `_id !== reviewId`. Thus, the new reviews array will not contain the review marked for deletion.

Running your App

When you run your app now, log in and go to a specific movie, a user will be able to delete reviews they have posted. We have almost completed the entire functionality of our app using the MEAN stack. What's left are some minor improvements to our app. Let's first see how to get the next page's results in the next chapter.

CHAPTER 25: GET NEXT PAGE'S RESULTS – SEARCH BY TITLE

Currently, we show just the first twenty results. We will add a 'Get next 20 results' link at the bottom to retrieve the next page's result (fig. 1).

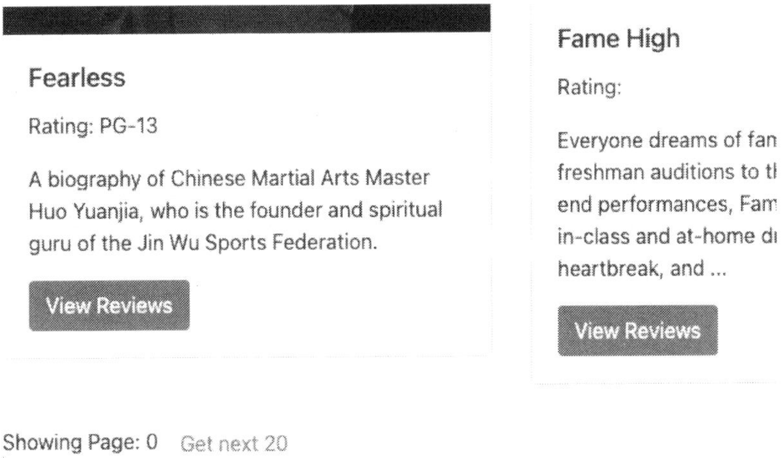

Fearless

Rating: PG-13

A biography of Chinese Martial Arts Master Huo Yuanjia, who is the founder and spiritual guru of the Jin Wu Sports Federation.

View Reviews

Fame High

Rating:

Everyone dreams of fan freshman auditions to th end performances, Fam in-class and at-home dı heartbreak, and ...

View Reviews

Showing Page: 0   Get next 20

Figure 1

Our code in the backend has already made it easy for us to retrieve results by page. If you recall, in *MovieDataService*, we have:

```
find(query: string, by = 'title', page = 0): Observable<Movies> {
  return this._http.get<Movies>(
    `http://localhost:5000/api/v1/movies?${by}=${query}&page=${page}`
  );
}
```

This allows us to retrieve the results of a particular page by providing the page argument. This is supported by *MoviesDAO* in the backend, where we have:

```
cursor = await movies.find(query).limit(moviesPerPage).skip(moviesPerPage
* page);
```

to retrieve the results of a particular page by providing *moviesPerPage* and *page*.

151

Getting of Next Results

In our *MoviesList* component *movies-list.component.ts*, add the following in **bold**:

```
...
export class MoviesListComponent implements OnInit, OnDestroy {
  title = new FormControl('');
  ratingsDropdown = new FormControl();

  movies: Array<Movie> = [];
  ratings: Array<string> = [];

  currentPage = 0;
  currentSearchTitle = '';
  currentSearchRating = '';
  entriesPerPage = 20;

  subscriptionRatings!: Subscription;
  subscriptionMovies!: Subscription;

  ...

  ngOnInit() {
    this.subscriptionRatings = this._movieDataService.getRatings()
      .subscribe((data) => {
        this.ratings = data;
      });

    this.title.valueChanges.pipe(filter((text) => text.length >= 3),
      debounceTime(400),distinctUntilChanged())
        .subscribe((value) => {
          this.currentPage = 0;
          this.currentSearchTitle = value;
          this.currentSearchRating = '';
          this.subscriptionMovies = this._movieDataService.find(value,"title")
          .subscribe((data) => {
            this.movies = data.movies;
          });
        }
      );
  }
```

```
getNextPage() {
  this.currentPage++;
  this.subscriptionMovies = this._movieDataService
    .find(this.currentSearchTitle, 'title', this.currentPage)
    .subscribe((data) => {
      this.movies = data.movies;
    });
}
```

...

And in *movies-list.component.html*, add at the bottom:

```
...
<br>
Showing Page: {{ currentPage }}
<button type="button" class="btn btn-link" (click)="getNextPage()">
    Get next {{ entriesPerPage }}
</button>
```

Code Explanation

```
currentPage = 0;
currentSearchTitle = '';
currentSearchRating = '';
entriesPerPage = 20;
```

We declare the *currentPage* variable to keep track of which page we are currently displaying. *currentSearchTitle* and *currentSearchRating* as the name suggests stores the current user-entered search title and rating respectively.

```
this.title.valueChanges.pipe(filter((text) => text.length >= 3),
  debounceTime(400),distinctUntilChanged())
    .subscribe((value) => {
      this.currentPage = 0;
      this.currentSearchTitle = value;
      this.currentSearchRating = '';
  ...
```

If a user enters a search term into the search title field, we set the value to *currentSearchTitle* and an empty string to *currentSearchRating* (which means user is not searching by rating).

```
getNextPage() {
  this.currentPage++;
  this.subscriptionMovies = this._movieDataService
    .find(this.currentSearchTitle, 'title', this.currentPage)
    .subscribe((data) => {
      this.movies = data.movies;
    });
}
```

We have *getNextPage()* which increments *currentPage* and calls *MovieDataService.find* with *currentPage* to get results for that particular page.

```
<br>
Showing Page: {{ currentPage }}
<button type="button" class="btn btn-link" (click)="getNextPage()">
    Get next {{ entriesPerPage }} results
</button>
```

Lastly, in *MoviesListComponent*'s template, we show *currentPage* to the user and provide a link button that displays "Get next ... results". When the link is clicked, it calls *getNextPage*.

With this, we have implemented next page's result for search-by-title. Now what about getting the next page's result for search-by-rating? Let's implement it in the next chapter.

CHAPTER 26: GET NEXT PAGE'S RESULTS — SEARCH BY RATING

Our *MoviesList* component currently has two modes of retrieval. One is getting next page's results for *search by title* which we have just implemented. To implement the same for *search by rating*, we add to *changeRating*:

```
changeRating(value: string){
  this.currentPage = 0;
  this.currentSearchRating = value;
  this.currentSearchTitle = '';
  this.subscriptionMovies = this._movieDataService.find(value,"rated")
    .subscribe((data) => {
      this.movies = data.movies;
      console.log("ratingsDropdown",this.movies);
    });
}
```

Each time user searches by rating, we reset the current page to 0 and the current search title to an empty string. So, at any point in time, we know if the user is searching by rating (*currentSearchRating* not empty string) or by title (*currentSearchTitle* not empty string).

In *getNextPage()*, we then add in **bold**:

```
getNextPage() {
  this.currentPage++;
  if (this.currentSearchTitle.length > 0) {
    this.subscriptionMovies = this._movieDataService
      .find(this.currentSearchTitle, 'title', this.currentPage)
      .subscribe((data) => {
        this.movies = data.movies;
      });
  } else if (this.currentSearchRating.length > 0) {
    this.subscriptionMovies = this._movieDataService
      .find(this.currentSearchRating, 'rated', this.currentPage)
      .subscribe((data) => {
        this.movies = data.movies;
      });
  }
}
```

We add the *currentPage* argument to the call to *MovieDataService.find*:

```
this._movieDataService.find(this.currentSearchRating, 'rated',
this.currentPage)
```

Notice that when user selects a value from the *ratings* dropdown and calls *changeRating*, *currentSearchTitle* is set to empty. When user types into the *title* field, *currentSearchRating* is set to empty. This thus lets the app differentiate the current search mode of the user.

If you run your app now, you will be able to retrieve the next page results whether you are searching by title or searching by rating. What's next will be to deploy both the backend and frontend so that users can access it over the cloud. In the next chapter, we will first do so for the backend.

* Refer to the source code (www.greglim.co/p/mean) to see the full code of *movies-list.component.ts*

CHAPTER 27: DEPLOYING BACKEND ON HEROKU

We have finished creating our entire app using the MEAN stack. Now, we will show you how to deploy your backend to the web.

We will be deploying our Node.js backend to Heroku's servers to host and run on the Internet. The backend will connect to our cloud MongoDB Atlas database. The deployment process is relatively straightforward and you can simply follow along the instructions in the documentation to deploy Node.js apps on Heroku (https://devcenter.heroku.com/ - fig. 1).
But we will still walk you through the deployment process in this chapter.

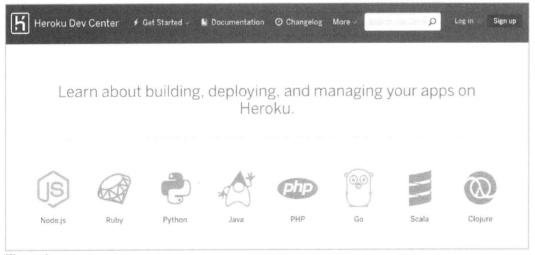

Figure 1

First, you will need a Heroku account. So, go ahead and sign up if you don't have an account.

Next, we need to install the Heroku Command Line Interface for creating and managing our Express apps on Heroku (fig. 2).

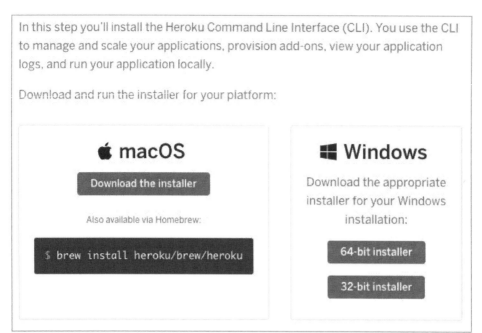

In this step you'll install the Heroku Command Line Interface (CLI). You use the CLI to manage and scale your applications, provision add-ons, view your application logs, and run your application locally.

Download and run the installer for your platform:

 macOS

Download the installer

Also available via Homebrew:

$ brew install heroku/brew/heroku

 Windows

Download the appropriate installer for your Windows installation:

64-bit installer

32-bit installer

Figure 2

When the installation completes, we can start using the *heroku* command from our Terminal. Type *heroku login* and a web browser will be opened to the Heroku login page (fig. 3).

```
$ heroku login
heroku: Press any key to open up the browser to login or q to exit
 >   Warning: If browser does not open, visit
 >   https://cli-auth.heroku.com/auth/browser/***
heroku: Waiting for login...
Logging in... done
Logged in as me@example.com
```

Figure 3

If the browser is already logged into Heroku, click 'Log In'.

Making our App 'Heroku Ready'

Before we start deploying to Heroku, we have to make our app 'Heroku ready'. We do so in the following sections by:
-    adding a Procfile
-    adding our Node.js version and *start* script to *package.json*
-    specify the *.gitignore* file

Add a Procfile

In our app directory, create a file named *Procfile* (capital *P*, without a file extension). This file will be run when Heroku starts our app. In our simple app, this file will only be one line. Copy the below line into *Procfile*:

```
web: node Index.js
```

web refers to the process type (the only process type that can receive HTTP traffic from the web). The command after *web* i.e. *node Index.js* is run on the Heroku server.

package.json

Next, add the version of Node.js that your app requires in *package.json*. That is, find out the version of Node you are running using *node --version*, and add it to your *package.json*. Also add the *start* under "*scripts*" for Heroku to start our app via *Index.js*.

An example is shown below in **bold**:

```
...
  "license": "MIT",
  "engines":{
    "node": "14.16.0"
  },
  "scripts": {
    "test": "echo \"Error: no test specified\" && exit 1",
    "start": "node Index.js"
  },
  "author": "Start Bootstrap",
  "contributors": [
    "David Miller (http://davidmiller.io/)"
  ],
...
```

.gitignore

Next, if we have not already done so, create a file *.gitignore* in our app directory. This file tells Git to ignore whatever is specified in it from being pushed onto the server. And because we don't need to push *node_modules*, add **node_modules** to *.gitignore*

With these steps, our app is now 'Heroku ready' and we can go ahead to deploy our app.

Deployment

For deployment, if you haven't already, you need to have the *git* version control system installed. Install *git* by following the instructions in https://git-scm.com/book/en/v2/Getting-Started-Installing-Git and then setting up *git* for the first time (https://git-scm.com/book/en/v2/Getting-Started-First-Time-Git-Setup).

When *git* is installed and setup, set up a *git* project in the app's root directory with:

```
git init
```

Next, use:

```
git add .
```

to add all of our project files. Then to commit the changes to your Git project, run:

```
git commit -m "Initial commit"
```

You will see in the logs something like:

```
Created initial commit 5df2d09: My first commit
 44 files changed, 8393 insertions(+), 0 deletions(-)
 create mode 100644 README
 create mode 100644 Procfile
 create mode 100644 app/controllers/source_file
 ...
```

Next, run:

```
heroku create
```

This creates a new empty application on Heroku with an associated empty Git repository. A new URL for your Heroku app will also be setup (fig. 4).

```
remote: -------> Launching...
remote:         Released v4
remote:         https://guarded-savannah-47368.herokuapp.com/ deployed to Heroku
remote:
remote: Verifying deploy... done.
```

Figure 4

You can change the URL or associate a domain name you own with the Heroku address but it is beyond the scope of this book.

160

Now, we push our code to the remote Git repository that we have just created with:

```
git push heroku master
```

This will push the code to the Heroku servers and setup our app's dependencies on them. Going forward when there are code changes in our app, run *git push heroku master* again to re-deploy.

And if you go to the URL generated for you and append */api/v1/movies* e.g.:

https://guarded-savannah-47368.herokuapp.com/api/v1/movies/

you will see the movies' data results!

In other words, previously, you accessed the API on your local machine with http://localhost:5000/api/v1/movies for example. Now, you access it using the URL Heroku has generated for you. And you can stop the Node process running on your local machine.

Changes to Frontend Angular Code

When we deploy our frontend Angular code, we must ensure any requests we are sending from the client-side is changed to use our Heroku generated URL now instead of localhost. Thus, change the hostname in your Angular frontend, *movie.service.ts* under *services* folder. E.g.

```
class MovieDataService{

    ...
   updateReview(data: any){
     return this._http.put(
     "https://guarded-savannah-47368.herokuapp.com/api/v1/movies/review", data)
   }
    ...
```

And also make sure that you are using *https* instead of just *http* as content must be served over secure *https*.

CHAPTER 28: HOSTING AND DEPLOYING OUR ANGULAR FRONTEND

In this section, we will deploy our Angular frontend to the Internet to share it with the world. We are going to use Netlify (netlify.com – fig.1) for our deployment.

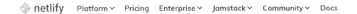

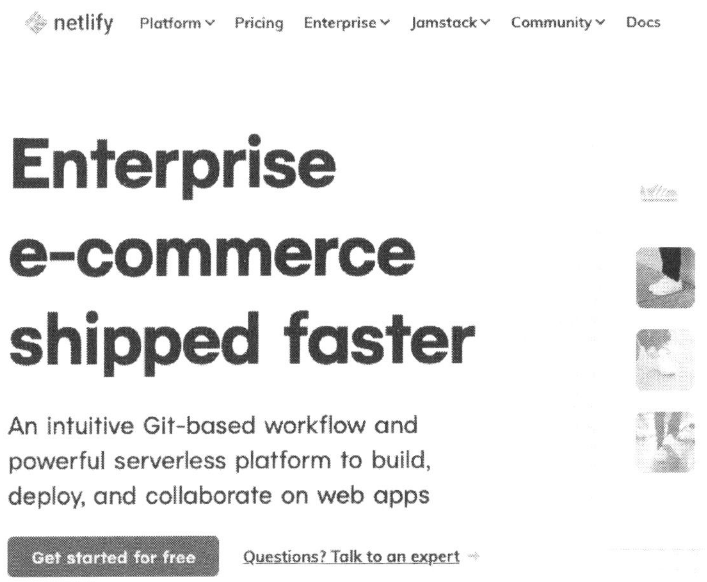

netlify
Platform
Pricing
Enterprise
Jamstack
Community
Docs
Enterprise e-commerce shipped faster
An intuitive Git-based workflow and powerful serverless platform to build, deploy, and collaborate on web apps
Get started for free
Questions? Talk to an expert

Figure 1

Go to netlify.com and create a free account or log in if you already have one.

When you log in, a list will show any deployed apps that you have. In your case, it will be empty since this is probably your first time deploying on Netlify. At the bottom, there will be a box with the message, "Want to deploy a new site without connecting to Git? Drag and drop your site output folder here" (fig. 2).

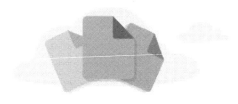

Figure 2

Go back to the Terminal and navigate to the *frontend* folder. Build your Angular application with the command:

```
ng build
```

This will create a build version of Angular that we can deploy on the web. When the build is finished, you will be able to see a *dist* folder in the directory.

Select the *dist* folder and drag and drop it into the box we saw earlier in Netlify. Netlify will take a few seconds and then generate a url where you can access the page (fig. 3).

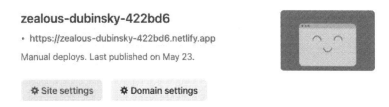

Figure 3

If you wish to have your own custom domain, you can go to 'Add custom domain' to purchase one.

And there you have it! Both your MEAN frontend and backend are deployed to the app, meaning that your fully functioning MEAN app is live and running.

Final Words

We have gone through quite a lot of content to equip you with the skills to create a MEAN stack app.

Hopefully, you have enjoyed this book and would like to learn more from me. I would love to get your feedback, learning what you liked and didn't for us to improve.

Please feel free to email me at support@i-ducate.com to get updated versions of this book.

If you didn't like the book, or if you feel that I should have covered certain additional topics, please email us to let us know. This book can only get better thanks to readers like you.

If you like the book, I would appreciate if you could leave us a review too. Thank you and all the best for your learning journey in MEAN stack development!

About the Author

Greg Lim is a technologist and author of several programming books. Greg has many years in teaching programming in tertiary institutions and he places special emphasis on learning by doing.

Contact Greg at support@i-ducate.com or http://www.greglim.co/

About the Technical Editor

Daniel Correa is a researcher and has been a software developer for several years. Daniel has a Ph.D. in Computer Science; currently he is a professor at Universidad EAFIT in Colombia. He is interested in software architectures, frameworks (such as Laravel, Django, Express, Vue, React, Angular, and many more), web development, and clean code.

Daniel is very active on Twitter; he shares tips about software development and reviews software engineering books. Contact Daniel on Twitter at @danielgarax